Sacred Masculine Energy

Unlocking Your Inner Strength and Connecting with the Divine Masculine to Achieve Clarity, Focus, and Balance

© Copyright 2024 - All rights reserved.

The content contained within this book may not be reproduced, duplicated, or transmitted without direct written permission from the author or the publisher.

Under no circumstances will any blame or legal responsibility be held against the publisher or author for any damages, reparation, or monetary loss due to the information contained within this book, either directly or indirectly.

Legal Notice:

This book is copyright-protected. It is only for personal use. You cannot amend, distribute, sell, use, quote, or paraphrase any part of the content within this book without the consent of the author or publisher.

Disclaimer Notice:

Please note the information contained within this document is for educational and entertainment purposes only. All effort has been executed to present accurate, up-to-date, reliable, and complete information. No warranties of any kind are declared or implied. Readers acknowledge that the author is not engaging in the rendering of legal, financial, medical, or professional advice. The content within this book has been derived from various sources. Please consult a licensed professional before attempting any techniques outlined in this book.

By reading this document, the reader agrees that under no circumstances is the author responsible for any losses, direct or indirect, that are incurred as a result of the use of the information contained within this document, including, but not limited to, errors, omissions, or inaccuracies.

Your Free Gift
(only available for a limited time)

Thanks for getting this book! If you want to learn more about various spirituality topics, then join Mari Silva's community and get a free guided meditation MP3 for awakening your third eye. This guided meditation mp3 is designed to open and strengthen ones third eye so you can experience a higher state of consciousness. Simply visit the link below the image to get started.

https://spiritualityspot.com/meditation

Or, Scan the QR code!

Table of Contents

INTRODUCTION 1
CHAPTER 1: WHAT IS THE SACRED MASCULINE? 3
CHAPTER 2: THE ARCHETYPES 13
CHAPTER 3: AWAKENING YOUR DIVINE MASCULINE ENERGY 29
CHAPTER 4: INNER STRENGTH AND COURAGE 41
CHAPTER 5: CLARITY OF MIND AND FOCUS 52
CHAPTER 6: BECOMING A LEADER 63
CHAPTER 7: ENHANCING THE CONNECTION: MEDITATION 75
CHAPTER 8: FINDING THE BALANCE WITHIN 84
CHAPTER 9: TOOLS FOR HEALING MASCULINITY 94
CHAPTER 10: THE EVER-UNFOLDING PATH 106
CONCLUSION 113
HERE'S ANOTHER BOOK BY MARI SILVA THAT YOU MIGHT LIKE 115
YOUR FREE GIFT (ONLY AVAILABLE FOR A LIMITED TIME) 116
REFERENCES 117

Introduction

The sacred masculine is the energy of action. There is a huge misconception about the divine feminine and divine masculine that constricts these vast expanses of existence to gender identity. Therefore, it is crucial to understand that the sacred masculine and feminine are the personification of timeless observations about the functioning of reality and the human condition. Everything in existence is on a spectrum. The opposite ends of some of these spectrums are labeled masculine and feminine for people to better understand the universe in a palatable and consumable way. Human beings express themselves and organize their societies according to their needs and biology. Although cultures vastly differ, some common understandings and behaviors are embedded deep into people's evolutionary history.

These expressions of humanity have been understood in different ways throughout the ages. Some use religion and spirituality, and in modern times, science and psychology are the lenses applied to these observations. Regardless of how you look at it, fundamental truths will be revealed when you begin to analyze these common threads. One of the most fundamental of these many truths is that consciousness and matter work together to manifest the reality in which people find themselves. Everything begins with a thought. Before a man and woman come together to make a baby, their relationship begins in the mind through attraction. This attraction is then acted upon through their behaviors, and if both people are on board, a child is made.

The thoughts that were the progenitor of the behavior are abstract and intangible, but the actions are more defined. This abstractness can be perceived as the divine feminine, while the solid and more tangible actions are the sacred masculine. This book will explore the inner work you can do, be it spiritual or psychological, so that the channel of masculine energy can be guided in a way most beneficial to you, those around you, and society.

Understanding the science of archetypes and narrative formation and diving into meditation and mindfulness practices will unlock the sacred masculine within you to its fullest extent. Everyone has a dream or vision within them. This book will teach you how to condense that vision into the external world from the abstract space through the masculine portals of discipline, self-control, rationality, focus, perseverance, courage, resilience, and strength.

By conscientiously applying the sciences of the divine masculine, you can take action to transform the world into your image. There is a huge responsibility to embody the role of the divine masculine because suffering and perseverance are part of the journey. This book prepares you for the hurdles you'll face when pursuing your dreams and desires while giving you the tools to mold life according to your imagination and internal reality.

Chapter 1: What Is the Sacred Masculine?

To understand masculine energy, you must first contrast it with feminine energy. Masculine and feminine on an energetic level fall into two Hermetic principles: the principle of gender and the principle of polarity. The principle of polarity means that everything within existence and its opposite are the same things being expressed in different ways. For example, hot or cold are both an expression of temperature and, therefore, are one. In essence, masculine and feminine are one expression of opposite polarities. This means that both masculine and feminine energy are the same in certain ways. The principle of gender is more closely related to masculinity and femininity because it outlines how everything within the universe has a feminine and a masculine expression.

Masculine and feminine are an expression of opposite polarities.
https://www.pexels.com/photo/silhouette-of-2-person-standing-in-front-of-white-and-black-stripe-wall-6491960/

It is easy to think that the sacred masculine means men and the divine feminine means women. However, this is a common misconception. If you limit your focus to humans, it becomes clear that men and women both contain masculine and feminine energy. At the biological level, half of your DNA comes from your father, and the other half comes from your mother. Both masculine and feminine are present for you to exist regardless of your outward biological expression. So, if feminine and masculine cannot simply be boxed into men and women, you may ask: what do these energies represent?

Unpacking the divine masculine requires you to first break down the words "feminine" and "masculine." When you analyze the word "masculine," you find that the last part of the word is "line." This hints at what masculine energy is. A line moves straight forward and goes directly from point A to point B. Contrast this with the word "feminine," and you'll find that the end of the word is "nine." Think of the number 9. Nine has a curve. Feminine energy is not as straightforward as the masculine. It works in waves, representing the more abstract part of the human identity.

Once you grasp that the masculine represents a line and a direct approach, its details can be further understood. The sacred masculine is all about taking action. The feminine is the internal work, while the masculine is the external. If you look at it through the lens of traditional gender roles, a clearer picture can be painted. In the past, women were expected to stay inside the house, while men were expected to go out and work for their families. Now, understand that this is not a promotion of traditional gender roles but rather a symbolic representation of how masculine and feminine energy function. Think of the home as your internal environment and the work that men go out to do as your external environment. Your emotions, thoughts, and beliefs that inform your actions are the feminine, while your expressions of your thoughts, emotions, and beliefs are the masculine.

The sacred masculine can then be broken down into how you engage with society. The divine feminine is the womb, while the divine masculine is the child. The child has to get pushed out of the womb to engage with the external reality once it is ready. Therefore, the sacred masculine is the mark you leave on the world. Another societal expression that makes masculine energy clearer is the tradition of a couple getting married and the wife taking their husband's name. The legacy of the external world comes through the paternal line or lineage. Take note of the words "line" or "lineage" as it relates to "masculine."

So, in a nutshell, the sacred masculine is about the imprint you leave or the expression of yourself to the outside world. The masculine is what you show, while the feminine is what you keep hidden. Another way to think about it is feminine is the darkness, and masculinity is the light. Light and dark in this context have nothing to do with good and evil. The light is revealing, while the darkness is all-consuming.

Qualities of the Divine Masculine

The divine masculine drive to action will be expressed in various ways. One of the primary ways that the divine masculine is manifested is through order, as opposed to feminine chaos. Too much order is terrible, just like an excess of chaos is detrimental. The key is to find a balance between your sacred masculine and feminine energies. Order is about rules, regulations, and discipline, while chaos is about free-flowing expression. Your divine masculine qualities will be expressed within a set framework: religious rules, political ideology, an ethical system, or the corporate world.

When you examine masculine qualities, attributes, and expressions, you find that they are all based on instituting or defending a principle or code. For example, strength is one of the first masculine qualities that pop into most people's minds. You are either going to use strength to build or to defend. The same is true for other masculine qualities like leadership, focus, assertiveness, and courage. Using your sacred masculinity to manifest the reality you want is not about these attributes or characteristics themselves but rather what vision you have that you are using these attributes to implement. For masculinity to be fully expressed, the feminine must be presented. Since the feminine exists in the abstract, your hopes and dreams can be classed under the divine feminine. However, for these dreams to grow out of the feminine womb, a seed must be planted, and this is where focus, leadership, courage, and assertiveness enter the picture.

The sacred masculine ensures that your vision does not remain in the void or the "womb." The divine masculine is meant to take on strain. When you neglect your masculine energy, your visions never come to fruition because you don't go out and get them. Overthinking is the main blockage to the manifestation of masculine energy. The most successful people in the world don't spend too much time thinking, but they do what needs to be done. Your fear can hold you back as you dance in the chaos of made-up scenarios. Using your sacred masculine means taking action and figuring things out with resilience and problem-solving. The masculine mind is analytical, so it is what orders the chaos of creativity. Think of creativity, which is required for your dreams and visions, as a wild horse. This horse is powerful and runs wild and free. Your analytical masculine energy comes in to tame and set it on a direct path or in a straight line. Masculine energy transmutes the abstract into the concrete.

The Misinterpreted Masculine

The misinterpreted masculine is what is typically referred to as *toxic masculinity*. This is when your masculine energy is out of balance with the feminine, so it spills over into a domineering and oppressive space. Misogyny and patriarchy are the consequences of imbalanced masculine energy.

The misinterpreted masculine comes from insecurity, *which is far from masculinity*. In some men, insecurity causes them to freeze up and not move to do what is needed. In others, it causes an imbalanced overcompensation, which gets expressed aggressively through the attempt to control – instead of *leading* others.

For example, a blue-collar worker may experience extreme exploitation and oppression at his job. As a result, he suppresses his masculine essence in order to assert himself and stamp his mark on the world – creating a feeling of lack. Due to this lack, he may go home and feel the need to overexert his power because his house is where he has some say in a world that suppresses him. This can then result in emotional, physical, and psychological abuse. The tyranny that he experiences in the exploitation, which is also caused by the misinterpreted masculine of wanting more without end, will then take root in his home, creating a chain reaction of oppression. The man may have a son who will now exert oppressive power over those that he can, like abusing a pet or bullying other children at school. The misinterpreted masculine is like a social rot or disease that infects everything it comes into contact with.

In a materialistic world with stereotypes, freedom from these chains is necessary.
https://unsplash.com/photos/man-in-black-suit-standing-on-top-of-building-looking-at-city-buildings-during-daytime-5BIbTwXbTWk

In a world where misogyny, patriarchy, oppression, and tyranny run rife, a masculine revolution is needed. Envisioning a world free from these poisons is not enough. The divine masculine has to propel you to take action. The divine masculine has righteous and wicked expressions. When this energy is tainted, it aims to oppress and control *instead of uplift and guide.* The misinterpreted masculine is a slave driver whipping people from behind to do his bidding.

In contrast, the actualized masculine is the one that leads their people from the front into a brighter future by being the example. The divine masculine has the perfect balance of competitiveness and cooperation instead of the misinterpreted masculine that wants to win at all costs, even to the detriment of others, including their team. The only way to be free from the distorted masculine is to grow from the healed feminine space of compassion, nurturing, and emotional intelligence.

Historical and Mythological Roots of the Divine Masculine

The divine masculine goes back to the beginning of time. The Genesis creation account in the Bible describes the earth in the beginning as formless and void. This is representative of the womb of creation. You can also look at it more scientifically when physicists describe the universe coming from nothing. Nothing can be represented as the womb. The formless void must be ordered through the masculine filter to create something. This is where the Biblical God, often personified as male, begins to take action and order creation with his words. These words represent a vibration or a movement to implement the change you want to see, which, in essence, is the basis of the divine masculine. Similar myths of the order coming out of the chaotic primordial waters are contained throughout various cultures' creation myths.

In mythology and fiction, the divine masculine typically manifests as one of four archetypes (or some combination of them). These archetypes are the **king, lover, magician, and warrior.**

The **king** represents leadership and overcoming hardships. The archetype of the king is trialed, and once he prevails, he earns his right to rule. He is primal and deals with order, honor, and virtue.

The **warrior** represents the destructive capacity of the divine masculine in mythology. However, the warrior's violence is to bring forth the greater good. He has an ideological background like a knight, so he is not consumed by mindless savagery.

A **magician** usually guides the king or warrior. The magician is the knowledge or expert expression of the divine masculine that takes a secondary position of support. He is extremely powerful, but he uses his power to uplift others.

Lastly, you have the **lover** archetype, which is about pleasure and worldly desires. The lover expression is needed in the divine masculine because stamping yourself on a world that you hate and gain no pleasure from results in destruction.

You see these archetypes being repeated in different stories, myths, and legends throughout the globe.

In the primal state, masculine and feminine energy were more closely aligned to their physical or biological expression, although there have been overlaps since the beginning. Asexual reproduction evolved before sexual reproduction. Somewhere in humanity's distant past - before people became human - they were unicellular organisms, so the masculine and feminine were more explicitly embodied in one being. The key concept of evolution is *survival of the fittest*, which, unlike many people, misunderstand it to mean it is not about force or strength. Survival of the fittest means those most adjusted or suited to an environment will thrive.

For whatever reason, nature chose to develop sexual reproduction to institute genetic diversity and make offspring more resilient to environmental changes. Therefore, humanity's oldest ancestors had male in female and female in male.

However, at some point when sexual reproduction and gender developed, nature called for more solidified roles for each sex. These roles carried into how societies were built and evolved with time according to the needs of mankind. The world has progressed so much that these gaps are closing. For example, the necessity for men to protect women is lower than it once was because of technological development and women being able to protect themselves better. The same is true for provision because women are also now in the workplace. It is becoming more apparent that either sex can embody masculine and feminine energy.

The next level of human expression is finding the balance that has been recorded in trinitarian mythologies of the mother, father, and child (like Auset, Ausar, and Heru in the Egyptian pantheon, or Shiva, Parvati, and Ganesha in the Hindu pantheon). All three are embodied within all people, and to be fully actualized, you must understand all of these expressions. This book only focuses on the divine masculine, though.

Male Identity Crisis

In the past, it was clear what was expected of a man. Feminist movements and the progressive shifting of societal attitudes coupled with accelerated technological development have placed women in spaces they have never been in before. These changes have disturbed the masculine energy within males because masculinity wants what is clear and defined, and in the modern context, the lines have become blurred. In past times, men protected and provided while women nurtured and cared for the home and family. These structures are no longer so clear-cut, especially in trying economic times where most households need dual incomes to stay afloat. This progress has unwittingly caused a crisis of masculinity where too many men have no idea how they fit into the societal structure. Unfortunately, it has also caused many toxic ideas and influencers to rise, especially in the online space with "alpha male podcasts" and the "Red Pill" community.

This redefining of masculinity for men does not have to be a crisis but can be transitioned into an opportunity. There is still so much wrong with the world and problems that need to be solved, which is where masculine energy works its magic. For a man to stand strong in the fullness of his masculinity, he has to do some introspective soul-searching to find out what he wants to be, how he relates to the world, and what mark he wants to leave on the planet. Once these questions are answered, a man can channel his masculinity to take focused action and confidently assert himself to shape the world and, more importantly, himself in the image of his vision. There is no longer a cookie-cutter mold of what it means to be a man, so there is freedom for you to bravely carve out a path into the unknown and stake a claim in the new world that society is creating together.

Where men were once given a masculine identity, it is now the time to create one. You don't need to listen to bald men shouting into a podcast microphone, trying to sell you overpriced scam courses about what you need to do to be a man! Sacred masculinity is about leading the way forward – but before you can lead others, you must guide yourself. Start with the mirror, then expand into your home, and then your community and build from there. The divine masculine is what gives you the power to shape the world like the people before you who instituted the roles that are now breaking down. Your mold of masculinity is decentralized, which puts a lot more of the power and responsibility in your hands to determine how you are going to manifest your masculinity.

The Fluidity of Gender and Inclusivity

There have been matriarchal and patriarchal societies depending on the time and region you find yourself in. Now, the world is entering a space of balance. The reorganization required to find this balance has questioned gender identities and how they have been understood, particularly in a Westernized context. Many are resisting this question. However, the ball is already rolling. How people understand sex, gender, and gender roles is rapidly shifting. This is the feminine period of chaos before the masculine period of order comes into play, so society is still navigating the unknown regarding gender identity and how people want to define themselves. Eventually, a natural equilibrium will be reached, but it will be way different than what the world has been conditioned to accept.

Sex and gender identity have become two separate concepts. One does not have to express the gender that aligns with their sex anymore. This shows that masculine and feminine are spiritual concepts that operate in the realm of energy that are only tangentially tied to biology. It is easy to box these concepts into man and woman when speaking of divine feminine and sacred masculine. People often think of it as women should exhibit the sacred feminine and men should exhibit the sacred masculine without understanding how limiting this view is. All genders embody the divine masculine because everyone needs to take action and move analytically at different moments in life. When you look at temperament, typically, men show masculine qualities more often than women, but no woman is free from masculine energy on a spiritual or biological level *because the seed and the soil are both needed to bring forth life.*

This book will highlight the psychological, biological, and spiritual overlaps, but the sacred masculine will be explored predominantly on an energetic and vibratory level. Your gender identity is irrelevant to whether you can embody the sacred masculine because that aspect is a part of all humans. As you dive deeper into the sacred masculine and understand how embracing it can benefit your life, you'll begin to realize that it is not your gender that drives you but your energy that gets condensed into the physical. By taking analytical action through the sacred masculine, you can construct your reality from the ground up by balancing the unseen and the seen in ways that will profoundly change your life.

Chapter 2: The Archetypes

Archetypes: The Jungian Connection

Carl Jung is considered by many to be one of the fathers of modern psychology. However, his work continued beyond the realm of psychology or how people would conceptualize it today. Jung explored mythologies and story structures as they relate to the development of mankind. From this study came the concept of archetypes. Jung described archetypes as common patterns and symbols that emerged from the collective unconscious of humanity. Because of this, you'll find similar story structures across cultures and times that get repeated as if they are embodied deep within the DNA of humanity.

Jung explored mythologies and story structures as they relate to the development of mankind.
orionpozo, ATTRIBUTION 2.0 GENERIC, CC BY 2.0,
<https://creativecommons.org/licenses/by/2.0/> https://www.flickr.com/photos/orionpozo/6914204764

Jung theorized that the collective identity functions at a lower form of consciousness than the individual. You then find phenomena like mob mentality, where people in a group do horrific things that they could never do alone. These tropes, or archetypes, are almost automatic and are probably sown deep into people's genetic past and evolutionary history. Studying these archetypes reveals deeply hidden driving forces that guide individual actions and how society is structured. In the light of the sacred masculine, which is driven by focused action, these archetypes show up in a variety of ways, both beneficial and detrimental. It can be enlightening to explore how archetypes present themselves in fiction and mythology and how they manifest in daily life. You will then be able to assess which archetypes you align with at different periods in your life so you can make informed decisions about how to maximize the greatness of the tropes you embody and integrate the shadow of these archetypes to turn negativity into positivity.

The Hero's Journey

The hero's journey is one of the two-story structures that every written work or oral tradition follows. An impactful narrative will either be a hero's journey or a tragedy. Tragedies are stories of the downfall of the capable and usually include how misdirected ambition can cause destruction. Tragedy is common in Shakespearean works like Macbeth or Othello. The hero's journey is something that most people get introduced to as children.

The hero story structure begins with the protagonist in his ordinary world, which then gets disrupted for some reason. He then gets a call to action to address this disruption. The hero will undergo some training and will inevitably fail at first. This failure will cause the hero to fight battles internally and address their shortcomings before returning to defeat the antagonist and restore order. Once the villain is defeated, equilibrium is reinstated, but the world and the hero are forever changed. This structure can be applied to many battles that people face in their lives. The beginning of the hero's journey is the call to action, equating to the activation of the divine masculine that begins unfolding as the narrative progresses.

The Symbology of Archetypes and Their Relevance in Your Life

In the Jungian understanding, there are four main archetypes: the **persona**, the **shadow**, the **anima** (or animus), and the **self**. From these four archetypes emerge the archetypal figures, which manifest themselves through narrative structures.

The *persona* is the mask you wear before the world.

The *shadow* is the parts of yourself that are repressed, yet they motivate many of your actions.

The *anima* is the feminine projection in the male mind, while the *animus* is the male projection in the female psyche.

The *self* is the combination of the conscious and unconscious of an individual. These four archetypes give rise to 12 archetypal figures embodied in real-world behavior and are used to tell stories. By exploring these archetypal figures, you can begin mapping yourself in relation to the world by expressing your masculine energy.

Each of these archetypal figures can be categorized into ego, order, social, and freedom. The ego is concerned with making your presence felt or obtaining some form of validation and admiration. Order is all about maintaining and establishing social structures. Social aims to build bonds with others – and freedom – is about overcoming physical and psychological limitations. The archetypal figures will have one of these categories as their primary motivation.

It is important to remember that you will not fall *neatly* into any of these archetypes; you'll most likely express many of them in your multifaceted life, even if one emerges as a primary identifier of your behavior. You may embody one archetype at home, another at work, and a different one in social settings. The archetype you most relate to may change with time and as you learn. Therefore, don't get too caught up with trying to identify with one archetypal figure, but rather see how all of them show up in your life to gain a deeper insight into your motivations so that you can use the divine masculine within you to direct your actions through the filter of these figures. These archetypal figures are not you but rather a map to navigate the infinite complexity of the human being.

The Innocent

This archetypal figure represents naivety and is an over-trusting individual. You may see this in films as someone who was sheltered or comes from a completely different world learning to exist in a new space. The innocent overlook threats and live in delusion due to their ignorance. They are pure of heart, and their negativity is not malicious but rather a result of their child-like misunderstanding. In fiction, you can think of Alice in Wonderland or Dorothy from The Wizard of Oz, who unwittingly fall into all types of dangerous and adventurous situations.

This archetypal figure represents naivety, like Alice from Alice in Wonderland, who unwittingly falls into all types of dangerous and adventurous situations.
https://pixabay.com/photos/alice-wonderland-mushrooms-fiction-6024906/

The shadow of the innocent is a complete denial of reality. That manifests as an over-optimistic outlook on life and can often be a burden to those around them who have to clean up the messes they make. The innocent is the embodiment of unfiltered righteousness. Due to their naivety, the innocent is easy to take advantage of. Forrest Gump is the perfect fictional representation of the innocent because his simple and pure worldview misses much of the darkness that occurs in the film. The shadow of the innocent can also show up as addiction or perpetual childhood due to being unable to accept reality at face value.

The tainting of the innocent is reflected in the often-told story of a child star that spirals. They enter the dark environment of Hollywood without the tools to see exploitation. This process can be seen with the spiraling of stars like Justin Bieber, Lindsey Lohan, and Brittany Spears. Integration of the shadow means bringing unconscious motivations into the conscious or shining light into the darkness. Taking masculine action to integrate the shadow of the innocent means keeping a playful spirit while becoming more aware of the danger of ascending from a child-like state. For example, a musician may keep an innocent and playful nature to make good music, but they should also study the industry's business side to prevent themselves from getting exploited.

The Everyman

The everyman is precisely what the name describes. This individual is the ultimate average and simply wants to fit into the role that society has carved out. In fiction, this is usually the character that is inserted for the audience to relate to. In Scott F. Fitzgerald's Great Gatsby, Nick Carraway is a perfect example of an average character who gets thrown into the middle of the extraordinary world of Jay Gatsby to act as the reader's eyes. In the context of the novel, Nick Carraway is seeking to fit into the world of the rich and famous that Jay introduces him to.

Nick Carraway is a perfect example of an average character who gets thrown into the middle of an extraordinary world.
https://commons.wikimedia.org/wiki/File:Neil_Hamilton_as_Nick_Carraway_in_The_Great_Gatsby_(1926).jpg

In their attempt to fit in, the everyman usually sticks out like a sore thumb. Their need to be accepted often gets them taken advantage of. Integrating the everyman shadow requires you to internally seek out the motivation for your desire to fit in. From there, you can make more informed decisions about what you will conform to. Another downside of this archetype is getting absorbed into the background. The masculine energy of assertiveness is needed to break the shell of the everyman and leave your imprint in any room you enter.

The Hero

Justice is the primary motivator of the hero archetype. The hero fights for what they view as right and, along their journey, has to evolve to bring forth this perceived good into the world. The shadow of the hero is the tunnel vision that creates blinders blocking out every perspective of morality other than their own. When manifested in the dark side, the hero can get so consumed by their idealistic view that they become villains. If you take the Hermetic principle of polarity to analyze a hero, you realize that heroes and villains exist on the same spectrum. Someone may feel that their cause is just, but the outcomes of their actions will overshadow their intentions.

The hero is one of the most common archetypes in storytelling, which is why the hero's journey is such a repeated narrative arch. An example of a hero in mythology is Heru from the Egyptian pantheon, which is the linguistic root of the word "hero." Heru fights Set for the Earthly throne that was usurped from his father, Ausar. Heru has to come out of hiding to face his father's murder. This is an amazing embodiment of the divine masculine principle because it shows how you need to come out of the darkness to face your battles. That darkness may be the idea in your mind that you have not followed through on literal isolation. The hero has to accept the call to action, which is the activation of masculine energy.

The Outlaw/Rebel

Robin Hood is one of modern culture's most popular outlaw or rebel embodiments. He rebels against the system and steals from the rich to give to the poor. The outlaw, much like the hero, is driven by idealism. However, instead of functioning within the boundaries that have been set out for them, they reject all the institutions they view as corrupt. The hero and outlaw duality is like Superman and The Punisher. Superman has strict moral guidelines that would appease the sensibilities of the broader systems, while The Punisher takes morally ambiguous actions to achieve his goals. Their intentions are similar, but their methods are entirely different.

A modern-day example of the outlaw archetype is "hacktivists." These individuals illegally hack into various systems to achieve a perceived positive political or social goal. A popular group of hacktivists is Anonymous. One of their actions was against PayPal, Visa, and MasterCard after they refused to work with WikiLeaks, who were leaking governmental documents showing corruption. The hackers crashed the sites because of their actions against the whistleblower platform. The shadow of the outlaw is a nihilistic outlook of all systems and a rejection of reform from within. Integrating the rebel archetype means becoming open to working with people with similar goals within the institutions they reject. The outlaw archetype is one of the bravest expressions of masculine energy because it means taking action against the norms of the society you function within, inspired by a moral code.

A modern-day example of the outlaw archetype is a hacktivist.
https://unsplash.com/photos/person-wearing-mask-flha0KwRrRc

The Explorer

The explorer archetype is a more self-centered expression of masculinity. The explorer is driven by adventure and independence, always looking to pave a new way. The mantra of self-determination consumes this archetype. The explorer archetype has been popularized in films like Indiana Jones. An explorer faces danger purely for the thrill of it. The shadow of the explorer is instability and the urge to always be on the move. It is challenging to build on such unstable ground. In reality, the explorer archetype appears in many ways, like someone who is constantly job-hopping or people who constantly travel, like the new modern emergence of digital nomads taking online jobs so they don't feel tied down. It can be difficult to establish strong relationships as an explorer. Therefore, integrating the shadow of the explorer requires grounding and connections to some form of stability.

The explorer is driven by adventure and independence.
https://pixabay.com/photos/compass-hand-lake-adventure-4891499/

The Creator

When you think of the creator archetype, think of artists, musicians, innovators, inventors, and everyone who brings forth something new into the world. The creator archetype, as the name suggests, must create. In fiction, one of the most popular characters that express the creator archetype is Tony Stark, Iron Man from the Marvel movies and comics. Iron Man is a brilliant inventor who finds meaning in creation. The creator archetype expresses themselves through their creations. When their morality or ideology shifts, their creations will change along with it, like a songwriter whose lyrics evolve as they mature.

The creator archetype expresses themselves through their creations.
https://pixabay.com/photos/guitar-player-music-guitarist-5043613/

The shadow of the creator is procrastination, self-doubt, fear of failure, and unfinished projects. Integration of the shadow for the creator archetype requires accepting that people may not love your work and embracing organizational skills to stick to set timelines. Fear and doubt are the killers of creativity. The sacred masculine is used to move beyond this paralyzing point of over-analysis and criticism to take action and create the work you feel called to.

The King

A king or a ruler's function is to instill order in a community or society. Since order and leadership are classed under masculine energy, this archetype facilitates a powerful connection to the sacred masculine. For the king archetype to be expressed healthily, there must be balance. Two shadows of the ruler can manifest negatively: the tyrant and the weakling. The tyrant is an authoritarian style of leadership where no one else gets a say and all freedom is suppressed, and the weakling is the pushover leader who gets swayed left and right because of outside pressure. The shadow of the king is integrated by finding a balance between taking suggestions and asserting himself.

A king or a ruler's function is to instill order in a community or society.
https://www.pexels.com/photo/close-up-shot-of-a-poker-card-5966408/

The destructive aspects of the king archetype are elitism, being overly controlling, and an aversion to chaotic spontaneity. Being too immovable can be destructive, like a tree that is too rigid to bend with strong winds. The ruler archetype shows up in any leadership role, including a company CEO, a team captain or coach, or a political leader like a president or governor. In media, a healthy king archetype is Mufasa from The Lion King, who leads in a stern but fair way, only dealing out discipline when needed, taking advice from his servants, and giving praise where it is due.

The Magician

A magician walks a tightrope between the seen and unseen realms to transmute dreams into reality. You can consider the magician as the bridge between the abstract divine feminine and the rigid, analytical, sacred masculine. When the magician shows up in narratives, it is often a male with a flamboyant flair related to femininity. The magician represents the balance between the two. The magician is often in the role of the assistant to a hero, helping them transform into their full capacity. In the real world, the magician will, therefore, be someone taking on the position of a mentor, advisor, or right-hand man.

A magician walks a tightrope between the seen and unseen realms to transmute dreams into reality.
https://www.pexels.com/photo/a-man-doing-illusion-6255279/

The shadow of the magician is their tendency to be manipulative and deceptive. This is because they understand that reality is not grounded in facts and logic but rather in narrative and perspective, so they play with these views. The magician plays with these perceptions either to teach or just for fun. King Arthur's mentor, the wizard Merlin, is a brilliant depiction of the magician in fiction and mythology. One of the most famous people aligned with the magician archetype is the literal magic practitioner Aleister Crowley. The controversial Crowley is loved and hated by many. He reshaped how the occult is understood and instituted some of the most widely practiced forms of ceremonial magic. Crowley also embodied some of the downsides of the magician archetype with broken relationships, drug abuse, and excessive pleasure.

The Lover

Aphrodite, the goddess of love in the ancient Greek pantheon, is a perfect example of the lover archetype. This archetype is based on chasing pleasure and emotional highs. Aphrodite never settles down with just one partner, instead moving between multiple lovers. Aphrodite is a sexual partner for half the males on Olympus, but there are a few narratives that get highlighted more often. The purpose of the lover is to find fulfillment in relationships.

This archetype is based on chasing pleasure and emotional highs.
https://www.pexels.com/photo/positive-black-man-demonstrating-red-heart-in-hands-6974956/

The lover's shadow is the objectification of others and the inability to establish a lasting intimate bond. They are always looking for the next high or more intense emotional experience by zooming in on the flaws of their current relationships and idealizing their next partner. To integrate the shadow of the lover archetype and take masculine action, you need to decentralize your passion for romantic relationships and place that on some of your other goals. Falling in passionate love with various creative or business projects can help you channel the lover archetype to promote productivity instead of emotional turmoil and unfulfillment.

The Caregiver

Caregivers are motivated by altruism and often self-sacrifice. Their selfless generosity is dedicated to uplifting their loved ones or society and maximizing their well-being. A masculine representation of the caregiver is Denzel Washington's character, Robert McCall, in The Equalizer. He puts himself in danger to fight Russian mobsters to protect the female protagonist, Teri, whom he does not know. The caregiver's shadow is the feeling of inadequacy that they are not doing enough for others and neglect their well-being.

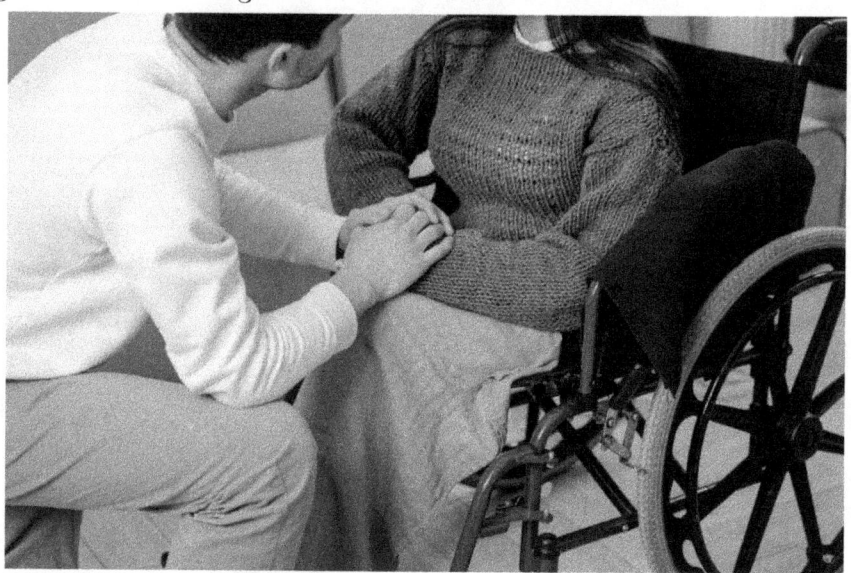

Caregivers are motivated by altruism and often self-sacrifice.
https://www.pexels.com/photo/man-holding-woman-s-hands-8127503/

In everyday life, people who strongly embody caregivers are the ones that others run to when they are in need. They often get involved in charities and can sometimes be easily manipulated by a convincing sob story. You need to establish firm boundaries to integrate the shadow of self-neglect that the caregiver has. The caregiver must set rules for themselves for whom they are willing to help and what kind of behaviors should result in them withdrawing their help. Furthermore, self-care is an essential aspect of existing fully as a caregiver.

The Jester

Another name for the jester is the trickster. Trickster deities have been feared, hated, and revered throughout cultures. In the Yoruba tradition of West Africa, the trickster deity, Anansi, is a shapeshifter that often appears in the form of a spider. Anansi is known for playing tricks on people that sometimes have dire consequences to either teach them a lesson, to get what he wants, as well as for entertainment or vengeance. Jesters tend to live in the moment and enjoy life without overthinking the past or future. The shadow of the jester manifests in the rejection of responsibility, and they can also fall into addictive patterns. You've probably met someone who aligns with the jester archetype, or you may fit into the mold. Jesters never take anything seriously but are always fun to be around due to their jovial nature. To integrate the shadow, people who relate to the jester archetype need to stay away from substances and, more importantly, learn impulse control. Jesters can use their ability to look on the bright side of life and view things more light-heartedly as a tool to solve problems.

Jesters never take anything seriously but are always fun to be around due to their jovial nature.
https://www.pexels.com/photo/a-person-wearing-a-jester-costume-6211894/

The Sage

Knowledge and wisdom are the markers of the sage archetype. A popular sage in fiction is Morpheus from the film The Matrix. Morpheus teaches Neo all about the real world and breaks him free from the illusions he was trapped in to reach his full potential. The shadow of the sage archetype is the need to always be objective and the propensity to be judgmental. Sages, in reality, usually are mentors or religious leaders. In some ways, the sage is the pinnacle of the sacred masculine because they balance study to obtain knowledge with practical application to gain wisdom. However, their certainty can alienate some people and break helpful social bonds. To integrate the shadow of the sage archetype, they need to be more forgiving and open-minded to subjective viewpoints by occasionally listening to others instead of teaching.

Knowledge and wisdom are the markers of the sage archetype.
https://pixabay.com/photos/man-portrait-beard-close-up-old-1851469/

Chapter 3: Awakening Your Divine Masculine Energy

The divine masculine is in a deep slumber. Constraints and uncertainty have led to the suppression of this essential world-changing energy. Some forces want a docile population that is easier to control. Therefore, your self-determination and masculine compulsions deeply embedded in your genetics, psyche, and spirit are being suppressed. Much work needs to be done to unleash the sacred masculine from the bondage it has been subjected to. By understanding how archetypal figures relate to you, mindfulness, visualization, and practices to integrate your shadow, your sacred masculinity can be unleashed to propel you to heights you never thought possible.

The divine masculine can emerge from within through mindfulness.
https://pixabay.com/photos/male-meditate-meditation-spiritual-5922911/

Identifying Your Dominant Archetype

Here are twelve questions. More than one may apply to you, but look within to see which one matches your personality the most. Ask yourself which of these you deeply resonate with, and it will help you determine your dominant archetype.

- **Are you ambitious, goal-orientated, and driven?**

   You are the hero archetype.

- **Are you orderly and organized?**

   You are the ruler archetype.

- **Do you love experiencing and discovering new things?**

   You are the explorer archetype.

- Are you drawn to creative projects like art, music, or inventions?

  You are the creator archetype.

- Do you enthusiastically love people and get excited about new relationships?

  You are the lover archetype.

- Do you have a nurturing and caring nature?

  You are the caregiver archetype.

- Are you easy to relate to and get along with many different kinds of people?

  You are the everyman archetype.

- Do you often study, learn, and research, and people see you as wise?

  You are the sage archetype.

- Are you daring and rebellious, constantly questioning authority?

  You are the outlaw archetype.

- Are you drawn to healing and problem-solving?

  You are the magician archetype.

- Do you love to entertain people and often make jokes?

  You are the jester archetype.

- Do you follow the rules and strongly desire to fit in?

  You are the innocent archetype.

Visualizations and Meditation

The first Hermetic principle is that all is mental. As the 17th-century French Philosopher Rene Descartes put it, "I think therefore I am." Your masculine transformation starts from within. Your mind does not control you because you are in charge of it. Yes, automatic actions occur in your mind, but you can tame them and direct them with sacred masculine order. Meditation and visualization are two of the most potent ways to begin reforming your mind. Now that you have identified your dominant archetype, you can implement meditations and practices that explicitly cater to your personality and temperament to attract the purest form of masculine energy and direct it to your benefit. Bear in mind that the exercises applied for each dominant archetype can be used by all people due to the multifaceted nature of humans. So, be open to trying various techniques regardless of which archetype fits you more closely.

The Outlaw

In its highest masculine expression, the outlaw takes action to overturn corrupt or unjust systems. For you to excel, you must visualize the world you want to create. Close your eyes in a quiet and safe space. Visualize the world you want to see. That does not necessarily have to be a grand global scheme. You can focus it on your household or community. Now, think about the institutions and actions you take that prevent this world you are visualizing from manifesting. Now, imagine how you can overcome and navigate the systems in the rebellious way that appeals to you and, most importantly, that brings you and society the most benefit.

The Magician

As someone who aligns with the magician archetype, you have an affinity for flair and theatrics. What is a magician without the explosions, the smoke and mirrors, or the showmanship? Your meditation as a magician aims to alchemize your reality from a space of imagination and enhance your guiding principle of wisdom. Your meditations as a magician can become more impactful with the use of rituals. Set up your space with candles, incense, colors, or whatever else you are intuitively drawn to. Candles are lovely meditation tools. Sit down with a candle in front of you. Control your breath and breathe in through your nose and out your mouth. Stare at the flame. When your mind wanders, bring your attention back to the flame and how the fire dances. After about 15 to 30 minutes of this, write down what first comes to mind. This gives you access to the hidden wisdom of your subconscious and will direct you where you can place the masculine energy of action.

The Hero

The hero archetype is goal-driven and idealistic. The visualization exercise that works best for this masculine manifestation is journaling. Plot a journey of where you want to see yourself in one month, six months, one year, and then five years. Write down how you'll reach your goals and which obstacles you'll face along the way. Think about the external factors that can stop you and which flaws within yourself hold you back. Once you have your success mapped out, place it in a visible position where you can see it every day. Measure your progress and make the necessary adjustments to the plan whenever needed. Gamifying your life this way channels the masculine drive to push forward.

The Lover

The lover archetype is playful and pleasure-seeking. To alchemize your masculine essence through this highly feminine representation, you must find a way to transmute the mundane into magic. The sacred masculine is about productivity. Since you are drawn to passion, you must find a way to insert that passion into your goals. A simple way of doing this is by naming your tasks and referring to them as if they are people. For example, if you are a mechanic who works on cars, you can give your projects names like Jessica or Stephanie. When you speak or think about your projects, reframe the tasks as personified in your mind, like "I'm going to spend some time with Jessica today. She's been giving me issues, but we'll work through it." This way, you can channel the lover archetype into your goals and projects.

The Jester

The jester archetype is a joyful spirit that finds humor in life. Jesters can be tricky and manipulative pranksters that can often stir up inappropriate trouble. One of the best ways to masculinely channel the jester energy is by using a laughing meditation to start your day and tap into the playful essence of the cosmic giggle. Start by standing with your feet hips-width, stretching your hand up, and bending down to touch your toes. Next, shake your body and relax your facial muscles. You can give your jaw a light massage to relieve any pent-up tension. Stand facing forward in a comfortable position and then gently smile. Begin with a light giggle for a couple of minutes. Progressively laugh louder until you reach the peak of the crescendo with an outright thunderous guffaw. Finish the practice by lying down and being aware of all the feelings in your body and thoughts in your mind. Write down your thoughts for guidance on what to take action on and to gain clarity about your life's journey.

The Everyman

The everyman's superpower is the ability to relate to many different kinds of people and thus advocate for them. Due to the everyman being susceptible to falling into the trap of being overly swayed by the whims of other people, their meditations must ground them in their own identity. Doing a body scan is a brilliant meditation for the everyman to become more aligned with themselves outside of their social identity, making them better able to serve the community. Start by lying down flat on your back. Take a few deep breaths, and imagine a bright light that begins at the end of your toes. As you continue taking deep breaths, imagine the light slowly moving upwards from your toes to your feet and up towards your calves. Take note of how each part of your body feels as the light reaches it. Feel all the sensations as the light passes over it. Imagine it slowly moving upward over every part of your body while paying attention to how you feel. Once it reaches your head, it will disappear, and you will feel more in touch with your being.

The Caregiver

The caregiver is the nurturing archetype that puts themselves second for the sake of their loved ones or everyone around them. As the caregiver, much of your life is dedicated to society and the community. Your deeply empathetic drive informs all your decisions. A grounding meditation helps the caregiver root themselves into the material realm so that their subconscious can awaken to how they will serve the world. Sit with your back straight and your legs crossed or stretched out in front of you, depending on what is comfortable. Take a few deep breaths, then imagine a root growing from the bottom of your body deep into the earth. When the root reaches the center of the earth, it will wrap itself around a large multicolored crystal. The root will absorb the grounding energy from the crystal and bring it up to your body. This energy will slowly fill you up from your feet to the top of your head before exploding outward into the world.

The King

As a leader, the king must always be aware of the needs of those that they are ruling for their decisions to benefit those who rely on them. It is easy for this archetype to become blinded by their rigid view of the world, so staying in touch with the community is important. Therefore, integrity and understanding are essential traits for the king archetype to embody. Affirmations can keep a leader on a beneficial path. When you are getting ready in the morning, take a few deep breaths and repeat these mantras to yourself five times.

- I am focused.
- I have a responsibility to those I lead.
- I am compassionate, grounded, logical, and intelligent.
- My decisions are the best for the people under my leadership.

- I am open to advice and am wise enough to know what to reject and what to embrace for the benefit of the people I lead.
- I am dedicated, unselfish, and perfectly capable of tackling all hurdles that come my way.

The Creator

The creator archetype's function is to bring the new into existence. Therefore, if you are a creator, your meditations and visualizations should increase your creativity and channel that energy toward positive action in a sacred masculine existence. This archetype functions best when they tap into the flow state, a condition where you are absorbed by the activity you are doing as the world melts away. To regularly enter the flow state, you must curate your environment to optimize your creativity. Institute a ritual for your creative process. For example, organize your tools, take a few deep breaths, stretch your body, and have a cup of tea. Then, jump into your work and don't allow yourself to get distracted. This ritual you create should be personalized to you, so think about what makes you comfortable and productive.

The Innocent

The innocent is a trusting idealist committed to bringing about their perceived utopia. The innocent can be misled or taken advantage of due to their naive nature, but their intentions are always pure. The innocent is dedicated to creating a better, more peaceful world. To gain external peace, the innocent must maximize their peace. Therefore, a negativity-clearing meditation is beneficial for the innocent archetype. Sit down with your legs crossed and back straight. You can also extend your legs forward if that makes you feel more comfortable. Take a few deep breaths to start your practice. While breathing, imagine a bright white orb ascending down from heaven. This orb is made of positivity. It comes down and settles just above the top of your head. As you breathe in, particles of pure positivity break off from the orb, filling up your entire body. Visualize these particles, gathering all the black and sludgy negativity in your body. When you breathe out, the orb particles carry out the negativity and disperse it into the universe. Practice this meditation daily for at least 15 minutes.

The Sage

Sages are personifications of wisdom. They study, guide others, and master themselves through dedicated practice. The sage is the wise old man who has been through it all and sees through the folly of the world using a compassionate lens. A meditative practice that aligns with the sage is memorization. In Islam's religious tradition, individuals known as hafiz memorize the Holy Quran so that if the texts are ever destroyed, the tradition lives on through their breath. Decide on a text that resonates with you. It does not have to be long or religious. Practice memorizing it or a section of it daily and recite it each morning as part of a meditation.

The Explorer

The explorer is driven by thrills, always wanting to discover new things. This bravery serves society because the explorer can bring back knowledge and practice from their journeys or adventures to serve those around them. This adventurous energy can sometimes get reckless, so you need your sacred masculine to direct it productively. It helps to journal about your daily adventures and discoveries so you can draw the lessons out of the thrills you seek instead of mindlessly spinning from adrenaline rushes. Every night before bed, write about what you did that day and what you learned. This can add order and meaning to the chaos of adventure, transforming your restless seeking into character-building productivity.

Tools to Integrate Your Shadow

The shadow is a complex concept that can be easily misunderstood. It is misinterpreted as the negative side of an archetype. However, this is only partly true. Shadows represent darkness and keep things hidden. They should not merely be seen as unfavorable; instead, they should be thought of as *all the traits, thoughts, and motivations* people suppress and hide from the world. When you think of a shadow as *negative*, you make the mistake of inviting its destruction. The shadow is a part of yourself that will always be there, so it can never be truly destroyed. You need to integrate your shadow to become fully actualized in your sacred masculine. That means bringing the hidden aspects of yourself into the light in a way that can benefit you and those around you. Shadow work is not about killing the beast but taming it so it can help you harvest in the fields.

The Outlaw

The outlaw archetype is also known as the rebel because they fight against established systems they believe are incorrect, corrupt, or unjust. The outlaw shadow can manifest as nihilism and arrogance. To integrate the shadow of this archetype, your value system must be deeply explored, and you need to be open to working with people who are reforming a system from within the boundaries of the rules and regulations of the institution.

The Magician

The magician plays with reality to manifest dreams in the waking world. In ancient times, the Shaman embodied the magician, who walked the tightrope between this world and the next. The magician's understanding of the abstract makes their shadow manifest as manipulation. To integrate this shadow, the magician must use their powers of manipulation to reveal more profound truths to people around them instead of controlling them.

The Hero

Since the hero archetype is goal-orientated, they can often have extreme focus and tunnel vision. Therefore, the archetype's shadow manifests as a dedication to the wrong cause. Their loyalty can cause them to take negative actions, believing that they are in the right, like members of a white nationalist or terrorist organization. Therefore, the shadow of the hero is integrated by regularly reassessing your perceptions, values, and motivations.

The Lover

The lover archetype finds meaning in relationships, passion, and the pleasures of life. The lover's shadow is manipulation and deception because of their need to constantly fuel their pursuit of pleasure. To integrate the lover shadow, you need to transfer your passions into your projects as opposed to relationships to minimize the harm caused by your unsteady nature.

The Jester

The jester highlights the foolishness of reality by playfully pointing out the silliness of what most people take too seriously through jokes, pranks, and tricks. The jester shadow is deception. They need to find a way to channel this manipulative deception in a way that benefits themselves and others so that they don't become alienated. For example, the jester can use their playful and deceptive nature to teach.

The Everyman

The everyman is a chameleon that molds and blends themselves to fit into society. The shadow of the everyman is the fear of not fitting in or getting rejected. To integrate this shadow, the everyman must search within what matters most for them. From that vantage point, you can find a group that matches your desires and values and fits into the models that they represent.

The Caregiver

Caregivers in the shadow become victims or martyrs to the service of others. The way the caretaker's shadow gets integrated is by setting firm boundaries. Caretakers are naturally inclined to self-sacrifice for the service of others. However, people can often take advantage of this kind nature. The caretaker needs to be strict with whom they share their loving nature.

The King

The shadow of the king or ruler archetype is an overinflated ego expressed in authoritarian proclivities. Nobody wants people to know they have a higher opinion of themselves than those around them. The unbalanced ruler may suppress their narcissism and egoic expressions from others and themselves, hiding behind rigid rules that they feel they follow the best. The integration of the egoic shadow of the king is to strive to be the best person you can be and then bring others around you up to your level. Instead of assuming they can never be like you, ground yourself in the reality that everyone has valuable gifts you can unlock through effective leadership.

The Creator

The drive to create can cause instability when jumping from one project to the next. The creator's shadow can manifest in harsh self-judgment and not being able to see how brilliant their work is. To integrate the shadow of the creator, you need to organize your time and make sure that you finish your projects. You'll always judge your work harshly. By overcoming that fear, you will find that their feedback is most likely not as terrible as your own.

The Innocent

The innocent's idealism and positive outlook can hugely benefit a world filled with darkness. However, the inability to live in reality and take responsibility manifests in the shadow of dependency. Thus, the unbalanced innocent can attach themselves to the idealistic views of a manipulatively abusive person. Integrating the shadow of the innocent requires the acceptance of failure as an opportunity to learn. Getting attached to different people or groups will result in your fingers getting burnt, but you must resiliently build yourself up from this as a dominantly innocent archetype.

The Sage

The sage is wise and often represented in mythology as an old man. Due to their understanding of the world, the sage's shadow can manifest as emotionally detached, rigid, and overly critical. To integrate this shadow, the sage must take on students whom they can learn from in their teaching relationships. Correcting a student is welcomed, but being hyper-critical of random individuals can be isolating.

The Explorer

The explorer's shadow manifests through their desire to always find something new. This creates escapist qualities that can become apparent through substance abuse or unfiltered thrill-seeking, which prevents them from establishing strong bonds. To integrate the shadow of the explorer, you need to turn the mundane into an adventure. This means finding new ways to do old things so that your mind is always engaged with the novelty of everyday life, which prevents escapism.

Harmonizing the Intersections of Your Archetypes

It is unlikely that the entirety of your being will just slip neatly into one archetypal figure. People are layered beings that function in multiple complex ways. Your archetypal expressions may be contradictory and paradoxical. The only way you can harmonize the intersections of the various archetypes you embody is by doing the inner work to identify which archetypes show up in which scenarios or contexts in your life. For example, you may embody the caregiver at home with your family and at work act as the ruler while being more of the jester in social environments. Understanding the layers of yourself requires mindful practices so you can sort through the mess of your internal environment and order it with the sacred masculine.

Mindfulness to Awaken the Masculine

In light of understanding the integrations of your shadow and the harmonizing of your intersecting archetypes, mindfulness is one of the most valuable practices that you can use to awaken the sacred masculine. Mindfulness means being present fully at the moment without judgment or attachment. This helps the sacred masculine because it can focus on one task at a time and push through until it is completed. Many practices enhance your mindfulness, but the best way to integrate it through the divine masculine into your life every day is by living in the moment and focusing on one task at a time. Meditation does not have to be sitting with closed eyes, crossed legs, and breathing while chanting a mantra. These mindful exercises are beneficial, but you can expand your practice by using your everyday tasks as meditations. For example, do not allow your mind to drift off when you are cleaning. When you catch your mind wandering, bring it back to focus on the task at hand. Being mindful then becomes a lifestyle instead of a practice, which gives the divine masculine space to develop and grow through disciplined control of the mind and asserted action.

Chapter 4: Inner Strength and Courage

Inner strength and courage are two of the most fundamental aspects of sacred masculine energy. They are two hearts pumping life into the divine masculine. Without them, the concept would devolve into nothingness and eventually transform into all the negative aspects of masculinity, like dominance and aggression. After all, the weak tend to be aggressive, and the cowardly need to assert their dominance. Before you get down to harnessing these two vital qualities, it's essential to understand their core meaning.

Inner strength and courage are two of the most fundamental aspects of sacred masculine energy.
https://pixabay.com/photos/fantasy-light-mood-heaven-lovely-2861107/

Inner Strength

Inner strength is your power that cannot be seen but felt. If used well, it can turn out to be one of the brightest areas of your divine masculine. It is mental and emotional, a unique energy flowing through your entire being. It affects three major parts of your sacred masculine energy:

1. Emotional Resilience

It can build your emotional resilience so you can respond to any situation instead of simply reacting to it. For example, if a long-standing, trusted client at work suddenly calls you and ends the contract, your initial reaction will be shock. Confusion follows, and when you are ready to face the client and understand their motivations so you can try to get them back, they are long gone. Emotional resilience allows you to recover from shock and confusion to proceed to salvage the situation.

2. Mental Fortitude

Inner strength develops another critical skill: mental fortitude. It is a measure of your mental toughness and resilience when your physical strength gives way. It is especially useful in sports and other physical activities. When you are playing soccer and have a clear shot at the goal but are completely exhausted and simply cannot take another step, your mental fortitude gives you the required energy to kick the ball. When you push yourself while working out, how do you manage to get in just another rep or run that extra mile each day? It's all thanks to your mental fortitude.

3. Perseverance

Perseverance, especially in the face of adversity, is a difficult skill to acquire. How do you keep going when everything is acting against you? How do you stand firm against an incoming avalanche of problems? Your inner strength kicks into action at such times, giving you the power to persevere so you can face any challenge head-on. It gives you enough strength to keep at it despite all the odds. The result may not always be in your favor, but self-satisfaction is assured.

Courage

Courage is not about being overly brave or immune to fear. It is about plodding on despite your fears. Fear is a perfectly natural emotional state, but courage is an acquired quality. The ability to face your fears and move forward is extremely powerful in people with a strong sense of the divine masculine. Courage can manifest in three different forms:

1. Moral Courage

This pertains primarily to your moral inclinations and is different for different people. When you are faced with a moral or ethical dilemma, do you stand by your values regardless of the consequences? Do you possess the strength to go against popular opinion? Moral courage is the ability to take a morally right action against all odds. For instance, if someone else is being reprimanded for a mistake you made, are you able to speak the truth? How about addressing an injustice in society when nobody else is doing so?

Moral courage is not easy to come by. People often prefer to go against their morality instead of standing strong, which makes sense in certain situations. You need to carefully weigh the situation's pros and cons before deciding. Moral courage isn't about impulsively or reflexively showing bravery. That's called a defense mechanism. Moral courage is all about thinking clearly and assessing the situation before taking action.

2. Physical Courage

This is the kind of courage you often see in action movies. When the protagonist keeps doing what's right without caring about physical hardships or death threats, they show physical courage. It is an endangered quality rarely found in today's world. Ask yourself the following questions, and answer honestly:

- Would you protect someone against an armed assailant?
- Would you rescue someone from a burning building?
- Would you prevent a crime from being committed when no one else is around?
- Would you report a crime under threat from a criminal?

If you answered "yes" to all these questions, your physical courage is right up there with action movie protagonists, which makes your sacred masculine energy shine intensely bright.

3. Confronting Inner Fears

Being courageous is not about being fearless but confronting your fears. Everyone is afraid of something. Your fear may be obscure, like being afraid of an octopus. You don't come across many octopuses in day-to-day life, so you simply ignore that fear. However, it still lingers within you, and you never know what form it may take in the future. The sacred masculine energy gives you the courage to face that fear head-on.

It becomes especially important if your fear is something common, like being afraid of heights. Don't find yourself in a situation where you end up at the peak of a mountain to face your fear of heights. Tap into your divine masculine energy and deliberately put yourself in a situation where you can confront your fears. This way, at least, you'll be well prepared for it.

In courage lies the secret to unlocking your potential to make difficult decisions. A number of new choices open up before you, ones you may never have thought about before. You acquire the power to make a difficult choice, especially if it is the right one. After making that choice, courage lends you the potential to go through with your decision without being afraid of the consequences. In short, it helps you take bold actions you may not choose to do under normal circumstances, like facing your fear of heights by climbing down the mountain's peak instead of waiting for someone to save you.

The Deep Connection between Strength and Courage

Inner strength and courage, the two pillars of sacred masculine energy, are deeply connected physically, emotionally, and spiritually. You will find the courage to undertake difficult tasks if you possess inner strength. Similarly, you'll find the strength for the purpose if you dare to face your fears; there isn't one without the other.

Say you notice a thief trying to snatch a passerby's purse on an otherwise deserted street. The thief is armed with a knife and is better built than you. You have the physical courage to take them on but not the required strength. Your common sense will prompt you to call the cops, but by the time they arrive, the thief would have done the deed and run off, maybe even knifing the passerby.

At this moment, as you muster the courage to confront the thief, your hardened resolve will lend you the strength to do so. Your emotional resilience will grow and prompt you to take action. As your physical energy drains, your mental fortitude will come to your rescue, and you'll find the inner strength to persevere. And who knows, seeing your courage and resolve, the victim might also help.

Scenarios and Contexts

How will you know when to show courage and use your inner strength? The scenarios that demand these two divine masculine qualities are not easily recognizable. You may have already used them in the past to tackle some problem or failed to use them because you didn't know you possessed these powerhouses of sacred masculinity. Here are a few relatable scenarios and contexts where you can implement your newfound powers.

Major Scenarios

- **You Have Lost a Loved One and Are Finding It Difficult to Move on.** Overcoming a trauma will be one of the greatest tests of your inner strength. Their memories may keep haunting you, and you may even (falsely) blame yourself for their death. Your inner strength will give you the power to let go. It doesn't mean you'll forget them. You will cherish their fond memories and celebrate their life, but their passing away will never hold you back.

- **You Have Failed Far Too Many Times and Wish to End Everything.** This will be the greatest battle of your life, for your life: you against you. Clinical depression is a serious illness that can be overcome with the help of the divine masculine. Two of the most effective medicines for hopelessness are your inner strength and courage. Giving up on life means you have lost the courage to live, implying that your inner strength is at an all-time low. Develop the strength to try again and gather the courage to fail again. Success won't be too far off.

- **You Have Experienced a Shocking Incident.** You may think that recovering from an accident is entirely physical. It is a proven fact in physiotherapy that your mental state of mind is equally important for making a full recovery. You are filled with negative thoughts and emotions after experiencing something devastating. Your inner strength holds the power to transform them into positive feelings, encouraging you to dwell less on the past and focus more on the future. In turn, your courage helps you face that shocking incident and accept your circumstances to begin healing.

- **You Are About to Do the Most Important Thing in Your Life.** It can be anything, from sitting for an interview for your dream job or launching your startup to breaking up a long relationship or marrying the love of your life. During these turning points in life, your inner strength is tested. You may have been ready to marry for years, but when that day finally comes, you may not want to go through with it. This sudden change is called a number of things, like pre-wedding jitters or nerves, and it is completely normal. One of the reasons it happens is because of your faltering inner strength. You are probably thinking about the future too much. Focus on your present, and both those aspects of your being will return.

The Little Things

You don't have to wait for major events to explore your inner strength and courage. Practice with the little things that you encounter every day. Building your confidence and resilience takes time to gather courage and strength.

- Walk to work instead of taking your car or public transport. A bit of exercise every morning gives you the energy to go through the day.
- When faced with any minor ethical dilemma at work, don't take the easy way out. Do the right thing. For instance, if your subordinates already have a lot of work on their hands and your boss gives you some more, try to do it yourself or explain the situation to your boss. Both these choices require inner strength and courage. The easy (and wrong) way out would be to assign the extra work to your subordinates.
- If you find a homeless person having a heart attack on the street, don't think twice before administering CPR or calling an ambulance. Apart from being your duty as a human being, the act also tests your inner strength because people normally won't do anything to help the homeless or weak.
- After a hard day's work, go home with a smile on your face. Don't bring your work home. Your family and children may have had to endure their own set of problems. Listen to their complaints and woes. Show genuine interest in what they have to say. It requires a different kind of courage to show genuine happiness when you are in pain.

Embodiment Exercises

Once awakened, your sacred masculine energy is relatively easier to maintain than the connection between your mind and body. Your mind strengthens your body and vice versa, but if your senses are not in touch with either one, you'll lose the connection and, in turn, the power of the divine masculine. Part of the reason why you cannot bring yourself to help your fellow humans or take morally sound actions is the lack of the mind-body connection.

Embodiment is the act of getting in touch with your mind and body and feeling the world through your physical, emotional, and spiritual senses. Your thoughts and your physical being are interconnected, and embodiment helps you explore that link. It can be something as simple as touching the space around you with the palms of your hands. Simple acts like these will help you forge a better relationship with your mind and body and, eventually, with your sacred masculine energy.

Easy Breathing

Breathing comes naturally to you, but when you focus on it, you get in touch with your inner consciousness, your mind. Practice breathing for a few minutes each day.

1. Breathe in. Feel yourself inhaling the positive energy around you. Imagine that it's boosting your inner strength and amplifying your courage.
2. Hold for a few seconds. Revel in your increased strength and courage.
3. Breathe out slowly. Feel the negative energy escape as you exhale. Let go of all your regrets, mistakes, and inhibitions.
4. Hold for a few seconds. Relish your freedom from the negativity.

Ultra-Focused Breathing

In this simple breathing exercise, you'll learn to feel where the air travels within your body.

1. Start with easy breathing. Get your mind to focus.
2. Take a deep breath. Feel the air travel through your nostrils, down your throat, and into your lungs. Feel your chest rise and your ribcage expand.
3. Without pulling up your shoulders, pucker your lips and breathe out slowly. Feel your belly contract as your lungs go back to their

original size.

4. When you think you can no longer exhale, use your belly muscles to blow out whatever air remains.

You'll have to deliberately repeat this twice or thrice, after which you'll naturally experience those feelings as you focus.

Grounding Techniques

These are similar to breathing exercises but are on a more physical level. Are incessant negative thoughts stopping you from connecting with the divine masculine? Grounding techniques will help you focus on the present moment instead of thinking about those negative thoughts.

- Use the 5-4-3-2-1 technique to get in touch with your surroundings. Acknowledge and describe five things you can see, four things you can touch, three things you can hear, two things you can smell, and one thing you can taste.
- Pick an object in your environment and focus on it. Pay attention to its color, shape, texture, and any other details. Close your eyes and try to sketch it in your mind's eye. This helps shift your focus away from distressing thoughts.
- Hold any object in your hand, like a stone, and close your eyes. Feel its texture down to the tiniest notch. Try to determine its shape. Is it oval or circular? Is it hard or smooth? Are there any jagged edges?
- Sit or stand comfortably and close your eyes. Imagine roots growing from the soles of your feet into the ground, grounding you. Feel the stability and support as you visualize these roots. Anxiety and negative thoughts often take over when you feel you have no support. This rooting exercise gives you that much-needed grounding support.
- Name or count the objects in your vicinity. Pick them up as you go for a better grounding presence. This helps you focus your mind on the present moment and takes your attention away from anxious thoughts.
- Close your eyes and take a few deep breaths. Imagine inhaling a calming color, like blue, and exhaling a stressful color, like red. Picture the calming color filling your body and pushing out the stressful color. This color breathing exercise is similar to easy breathing but more imaginative.

- Close your eyes and visualize a peaceful place. Engage all your senses in this visualization, imagining the sights, sounds, smells, and textures. How do the trees look, the flowers smell, and the fruits taste? What does the surface you're standing on feel like? How high-pitched are the birds' sounds?

Emotional and Spiritual Body Check

This is a slightly more advanced technique. It involves focusing on each part of your body, identifying the stressful areas, and de-stressing them. Start by focusing on your head. Take a deep breath and see if you notice any tension in your head or face. Do your eyes feel jittery? Are your lips pursed too tightly? Is there a bit of pain in your forehead? As you identify each stressor, try to release that tension and untie those knots with steady breathing. Repeat the same exercise with your throat, chest, diaphragm, belly, and pelvis.

Yoga

Embodied yoga is an approach that emphasizes the integration of mind and body, bringing awareness to the present moment through movement, breath, and mindful awareness. It goes beyond the physical postures (asanas) commonly associated with yoga and focuses on cultivating a deep connection with your body, sensations, and emotions. You have to focus not only on your breath but also on every part of your body. It ensures that you develop physical as well as inner strength. Two easy asanas (poses/exercises) you can try are:

- **Virabhadrasana (Warrior Pose):** It's similar to the lunges exercise, with one leg bent in the front and the other leg stretched behind. Keep your upper body perpendicular to the ground and your arms stretched upward. Hold this pose for as long as you can.

Warrior pose.
Gahlotyoga, CC BY-SA 4.0 <https://creativecommons.org/licenses/by-sa/4.0>, via Wikimedia Commons: https://commons.wikimedia.org/wiki/File:Ashish_veerbhadrasana.jpg

- **Tadasana (Mountain Pose):** This is almost the same as stretching your body while standing. With the fingers of both your hands interlocked above your head, stretch yourself as far as you can without bending backward. Stand on your toes to facilitate a better stretch.

Mountain pose.
Satheesan.vn, CC BY-SA 3.0 <https://creativecommons.org/licenses/by-sa/3.0>, via Wikimedia Commons: https://commons.wikimedia.org/wiki/File:Mountain_Pose.jpg

You can ideally do this with any other type of exercise, like tai chi or kung fu.

Chapter 5: Clarity of Mind and Focus

During your spiritual and personal development journey, following the divine masculine archetype can instill qualities that embody strength, decisiveness, and purpose. Likewise, having a conscious mind and excellent focus is necessary to develop these divine masculine abilities, become self-aware, and live a good life.

Having a conscious mind can be understood as your heightened state of awareness where your conscious and subconscious mind remains unclouded by confusion or distraction. This state of mental lucidity allows you to navigate thoughts and emotions with precision, unveiling a deeper understanding of life's purpose and values. When embodying the divine masculine archetype, your clarity of mind becomes the torchbearer, illuminating the path toward meaningful existence.

A conscious mind and excellent focus are necessary to develop these divine masculine abilities.
https://www.pexels.com/photo/man-in-black-crew-neck-t-shirt-sitting-on-brown-sofa-4553272/

Similarly, focus on a divine masculine context is the ability to concentrate on tasks and a strong commitment to undivided attention toward purposeful goals and milestones. It's the focus that will allow you to channel your mental energy into specific goals, cut through the clutter, and be determined to pursue your aspirations and objectives with unwavering intent.

In this chapter, you'll read about direct attention, purposeful action, concentration on meaningful objectives, decisiveness in decision-making, and harmonization with higher values to improve your clarity and focus. You'll also learn the neurological intricacies and psychological dynamics that underpin these virtues, providing a comprehensive understanding of how they can shape your journey toward spiritual and personal fulfillment.

Directed Attention

It's the intentional focus on mental energy towards a certain task or goal. It's a cognitive process (learning process) where you consciously choose to concentrate on a particular activity, filtering out irrelevant stimuli and inhibiting distractions. This cognitive process relies on the brain's executive functions, particularly the prefrontal cortex, which is involved in decision-making and sustained attention. Neurotransmitters like dopamine aid in regulating attention, and the brain's neural networks adapt to reinforce the chosen focus. This deliberate act of attentional control enables you to engage more with the present moment, enhancing cognitive performance and promoting a sense of mindfulness.

Purposeful Action

It's a deliberate behavior fueled by a clear understanding of your core values and overarching goals. This involves consciously aligning actions with a higher purpose or meaningful objective. Neurologically, purposeful action is linked to the region in the brain responsible for goal-setting and the reward system. The brain's ventral striatum responds to the anticipation of rewards associated with purposeful actions, making the connection stronger between your behavior and intrinsic motivations. Likewise, the prefrontal cortex, responsible for decision-making, planning, and self-control, shapes purposeful actions by integrating long-term goals with immediate choices.

Concentration on Meaningful Goals

An understanding of personal values and unwavering commitment is necessary to concentrate on meaningful objectives and goals. When you are determined to perform a task or strive to achieve a goal, the goal-related neural circuits activate in the dorsal lateral prefrontal cortex, an area associated with cognitive control and working memory. Besides the activation of these neural circuits, the brain's reward system activates, releasing neurotransmitters like serotonin and endorphins to reinforce the sense of accomplishment associated with progress toward meaningful goals. Furthermore, cognitive flexibility, facilitated by the anterior cingulate cortex, allows you to adapt your strategies when faced with challenges, maintaining focus on the overarching objectives.

Decisiveness in Decision-Making

Decisiveness is all about making prompt and confident decisions, unencumbered by indecision or doubt. At a neural level, decision-making involves various brain regions like the orbitofrontal cortex, which evaluates options based on reward and punishment, and the amygdala, responsible for processing emotions related to choices. The intricate balance between these regions, connected through neural pathways, leads to decisive decision-making. The hippocampus also becomes active, integrating past experiences into refining decision-making and ensuring adaptability.

Harmonizing with Higher Values

Harmonizing with higher values changes your ego for good, aligning actions with universal principles like the ones instilled in the divine masculine archetype. In medical terms, cognitive processes like these engage areas of the brain associated with social cognition, empathy, and moral reasoning. Likewise, the mirror neuron system makes you resonate with the experiences and emotions of others, promoting interconnectedness. The prefrontal cortex is also actively involved in moral decision-making, guiding you to make choices that contribute to the greater good. The brain's reward system further promotes intrinsic satisfaction when your actions match with higher values, creating a sense of fulfillment and purpose.

Each aspect of focus and clarity of mind within the framework of the divine masculine involves intricate neurological processes, engaging various brain regions, neurotransmitters, and cognitive functions. Understanding these mechanisms reveals a comprehensive view of how the mind navigates directed attention, purposeful action, concentration on goals that matter, and decisiveness in decision-making, all in harmony with higher values.

Common Mental Obstacles and Strategies for Overcoming Challenges

Procrastination

This is one of the most problematic obstacles that keeps you from growing, transforming, and giving things your all. Procrastination results from a mix of psychological factors, which mostly include the fear of failure, perfectionism, or a lack of motivation. The brain's limbic system, responsible for regulating emotions, deals with procrastination by triggering avoidance behaviors and minimizing the negative effects associated with challenging tasks.

Strategies for Dealing with Procrastination

- **Temporal Motivation Theory:** This theory states that the motivation you harness to do a certain task is influenced by the perceived value of the task and your expectancy of success. In simple words, the more confidence you have in succeeding, the more motivated you'll be to do the task.

- **Implementation Intention**: This strategy is based on forming a solid plan by specifying when, where, and how a task will be accomplished. You'll be using your prefrontal cortex to brainstorm and create a mental script to streamline the initiation of a task.
- **Cognitive Restructuring**: Rewiring your brain by addressing irrationality helps reshape negative thought patterns, contributing positively to procrastination. In cognitive restructuring, you'll face self-defeating thoughts and replace them with realistic and positive ones.

Self-Doubt

It's a cognitive phenomenon where you doubt your abilities and see them in a negative light. Past failures, perceived inadequacies, and fear of judgment mostly trigger self-doubt. The amygdala triggers self-doubt responses, sometimes taking you on an emotional rollercoaster.

Strategies for Dealing with Self-Doubt

- **Positive Affirmations**: According to psychology, listening, reading, and repeating positive affirmations stimulate the reward center in the brain, releasing dopamine and reinforcing positive self-perceptions. Neural pathways in the brain can be reshaped over time to counteract self-doubt through tailored positive affirmations. When searching for positive affirmations, pick the ones that align with the most important things and the core values.
- **Visualization Techniques**: This technique involves training your motor and visual cortex, training the brain by creating a mental rehearsal of success. Vividly imagining positive outcomes fosters a sense of self-efficacy, activating areas associated with confidence and motivation.
- **Self-Compassion Practices**: This practice includes drawing from principles of self-compassion, treating yourself with the same kindness and understanding you would offer to a friend. Being self-compassionate triggers soothing effects, reducing the impact of self-critical thoughts.

Distractions

There are two types of distractions: external, which includes any stimuli in the environment, and internal, which mostly consists of your thoughts. The brain's prefrontal cortex is the region responsible for regulating attention and maintaining focus.

Strategies for Dealing with Distractions

- **Reorganizing environments**: Optimizing your surroundings at home and your workspace can reduce visual and auditory stimuli that may divert your attention. Environments with low auditory and visual stimuli calm the brain's processing areas and aid in sustaining focus.
- **Task-Switching Costs**: The brain incurs a cost when switching between tasks. Recognize the toll you will be paying when switching tasks and encourage yourself to focus on a single task for more extended periods, promoting efficiency and minimizing mental fatigue.

Lack of Clear Goals

Without clear goals, you won't be motivated as much, and your actions may show a lack of direction. The brain's frontal lobes, responsible for executive functions like goal-setting, can struggle to initiate actions when objectives are ambiguous.

Strategies for Dealing with a Lack of Clear Goals

- **Executive Function Activation**: The prefrontal cortex can activate executive functions when clear goals are set. Clearly defining goals and breaking them down into achievable and actionable steps keeps the prefrontal cortex stimulated, facilitating clearer decision-making and sustained motivation. As you've read earlier in this chapter, your brain's reward center will also respond to these clear goals, releasing dopamine and reinforcing motivation.
- **Goal Visualization**: Similar to self-doubt strategies, visualizing yourself achieving goals creates a positive feedback loop that reinforces goal-directed behaviors. Your understanding of these mental obstacles and implementing strategies to cope with these issues will eventually lead to a more focused and resilient mindset.

Mental Clarity and Health

It's a no-brainer that physical well-being and mental clarity are interconnected. If there's an issue with your health, your mental focus, attention, and thought patterns won't be the same. Fortunately, various lifestyle practices like adequate exercise, balanced nutrition, enough sleep, and several others can be incorporated into daily life to promote mental and physical well-being.

Exercise and Mental Clarity

When you exercise regularly, mental clarity and cognitive function improve. Besides pumping the muscles and increasing blood flow to the heart to make it stronger, exercise triggers the release of neurotransmitters, including dopamine and serotonin. These neurotransmitters regulate mood and enhance attention. While brisk walking, jogging, or a workout will work, incorporating aerobic exercises in your routine promotes blood flow to the brain, delivering the essential nutrients for optimal cognitive performance.

Nutrition and Cognitive Function

Proper nutrition is fundamental for sustaining energy levels and supporting cognitive function. The brain requires a balanced supply of nutrients, including omega-3 fatty acids, antioxidants, vitamins, and minerals. Foods rich in these nutrients, like fatty fish, fruits, vegetables, and whole grains, must be included for optimal brain health. Just like you'll add these nutritious foods to your diet, avoid excessive consumption of processed foods, sugar, and caffeine to prevent energy crashes and support sustained mental focus.

Adequate Rest and Cognitive Performance

Quality sleep is indispensable for mental clarity and cognitive function. During sleep, the brain undergoes various processes like memory consolidation, neural repair, and toxin removal. Lack of sufficient sleep will only impair attention, decision-making, and problem-solving abilities. Try establishing a consistent sleep schedule, creating a conducive sleep environment, and practicing relaxation techniques for a restful and rejuvenating sleep.

Hydration and Cognitive Function

Dehydration has noticeable effects on cognitive function. Even mild dehydration makes it difficult to concentrate and increases fatigue. Staying adequately hydrated provides the brain with a constant supply of necessary fluids to maintain optimal function.

Stress Management and Mental Clarity

Chronic stress can detrimentally impact mental clarity, leading to cognitive fatigue and impaired decision-making. Practices like mindfulness meditation, deep breathing exercises, and progressive muscle relaxation effectively reduce stress levels and can be incorporated into your exercise routine for better stress management. These soothing techniques activate the parasympathetic nervous system, promoting a sense of calm and clarity in the mind. You'll read about these practices in detail in the mindful practices section.

Regular Breaks and Cognitive Renewal

Lastly, regular breaks during work or study sessions are essential for preventing mental fatigue and sustaining focus. The brain operates optimally in cycles of focused activity followed by short breaks. You can include activities like stretching, walking, and even taking naps when necessary to rejuvenate the mind, priming it to perform the next task with enhanced mental clarity.

The body and mind are intricately connected. Maintaining mental clarity is foundational to taking care of and enhancing your physical well-being. A holistic approach works best as it combines regular exercise, balanced nutrition, sufficient rest, stress management, hydration, and mindful breaks.

Mindfulness Practices

Stress Reduction

Mindfulness practices are well-known for their stress-reducing benefits. Deep breathing and various forms of meditation can activate the body's relaxation response, leading to a decrease in stress hormones. This reduced stress facilitates mental clarity by alleviating the mental fog associated with heightened stress levels.

Besides stress reduction, you'll develop stress resilience when you have a heightened awareness of thoughts and emotions. This resilience enables a calm and composed mindset, preventing stress from derailing your mental clarity and navigating challenges.

Emotional Regulation

One of the foundational pillars of mindfulness practices is to analyze your observations and thoughts without judgment. This practice takes you to a higher state of mental awareness, allowing you to regulate emotions more effectively. The emotional stability you'll harness from this practice gives you mental clarity and prevents overwhelming emotions from clouding judgment and decision-making.

Enhanced Creativity

Moments of stillness provide a fertile ground for creativity to flourish. You can access novel ideas and solutions by quieting the mind and allowing it to wander without external distractions. This creative enhancement contributes to a more expansive and innovative perspective, ultimately benefiting mental clarity.

Increased Self-Awareness

Mindfulness practices promote self-awareness by encouraging you to observe your thoughts, feelings, and behaviors without attachment. Staying in the present moment reduces the tendency to become distracted by irrelevant thoughts or external stimuli. As a result, channeling attention becomes easier and more effective. This heightened self-awareness allows for a clearer understanding of personal values, goals, and motivations, guiding actions and decisions with greater purpose and intention.

Enhanced Decision-Making

Clear moments of stillness provide a mental space where you can approach decision-making with a calm and focused mind. By reducing mental clutter and external noise, you can make decisions more thoughtfully and with greater clarity, resulting in more informed and strategic choices.

Improved Sleep Quality

Meditation and mindfulness practices that involve relaxation techniques can exponentially improve sleep quality. Adequate and quality sleep is vital for a clear mind and cognitive functions. You can create a short meditation routine before bedtime to improve your sleep experience.

These practical and effective practices offer a holistic sense of well-being. Incorporate mindfulness practices to enhance focus, improve mental clarity, and reduce stress to experience an improved quality of life. This sense of well-being permeates various aspects of daily living, promoting a positive outlook and a resilient mindset.

Getting Inspired

Drawing inspiration from masculine archetypes adds a rich and symbolic dimension when you are striving to achieve a heightened state of focus and a clear understanding of your path and life purpose. Here are some examples of archetypal figures to draw inspiration from and set your path toward achieving ultimate focus and clarity of mind.

The Sage's Wisdom and Insight

Understanding Inner Wisdom

The Sage archetype, deeply rooted in various cultural and mythological traditions, represents the embodiment of wisdom and insight. To draw inspiration from the Sage for mental clarity, you can delve into practices that cultivate inner wisdom. Meditation, a cornerstone of many ancient traditions, allows for a profound exploration of the mind's depths. Regular meditation gives you access to their inner well of knowledge and intuition, contributing to heightened mental clarity.

Seeking Purpose-Driven Knowledge

The Sage's pursuit of knowledge is purpose-driven. Instead of merely accumulating facts, you can adopt a mindset akin to the Sage by seeking knowledge that aligns with your life purpose. This purpose-driven quest ensures that every piece of acquired wisdom has relevance and contributes to a clear understanding of one's path.

Reflective Practices for Clarity

The Sage often engages in reflective practices to distill wisdom from life experiences. Emulating this archetype involves incorporating journaling, philosophical contemplation, or discussions with wise mentors into daily life. These practices encourage introspection and self-awareness, facilitating a clear understanding of personal values and the path forward.

The Warrior's Concentrated and Determined Mindset

Focused Attention on Goals

The Warrior archetype exemplifies concentrated determination. In the context of mental clarity, you can adopt a Warrior's mindset by setting clear and compelling goals. This focused attention on specific objectives eliminates distractions and creates a mental environment conducive to concentration and purposeful action.

Discipline and Routine

Warriors are renowned for their discipline and commitment to rigorous training. Translating this into daily life involves establishing disciplined routines. Whether it's a structured work schedule, a consistent physical exercise regimen, or dedicated mindfulness practices, routines instill discipline and build the mental resilience necessary for sustained concentration.

Overcoming Obstacles with Resilience

The Warrior faces challenges with resilience and courage. Applying this mindset means viewing obstacles as opportunities for growth rather than insurmountable barriers. This perspective shifts the focus from problems to solutions, contributing to mental clarity by cultivating a proactive and determined approach to life's challenges.

The Explorer's Curiosity and Adaptability

Curiosity as a Driving Force

The Explorer archetype embodies an insatiable curiosity and a thirst for adventure. To harness this quality for mental clarity, you can approach life with a curious mindset. Actively seeking new ideas, experiences, and perspectives stimulates the mind, preventing stagnation and contributing to a continuous learning process that fosters mental clarity.

Adaptability in the Face of Change

Explorers thrive in diverse environments and easily adapt to change. Applying this quality involves developing adaptability in response to life's changes. An adaptable mindset supports mental clarity by minimizing resistance to change. Instead of being overwhelmed by uncertainty, with an Explorer's adaptability, you can navigate the twists and turns of their path with resilience and an open mind.

Integrating elements from the Sage, Warrior, and Explorer archetypes involves a profound journey of self-discovery and intentional practice. Through meditation, purpose-driven knowledge-seeking, disciplined routines, resilience in the face of challenges, and a curiosity-driven approach to life, you can cultivate a mindset that aligns with these archetypal qualities, contributing to extreme mental clarity and a purposeful life journey. Although it will take time to understand the intricacies and develop an inner personality that portrays the earlier mentioned qualities and to achieve the purpose in life you aim for.

Chapter 6: Becoming a Leader

Effective leadership is a dynamic concoction of qualities and traits beyond mere managerial skills. A successful leader perfectly balances traits like strength, vision, and decision-making with integrity, humility, and empathy. They develop and strive to incorporate attributes that contribute to their ability to inspire and guide others. In this chapter, you'll read about key qualities associated with successful leaders, exploring the nuances and interconnections that leave an impact. Understanding the intricacies of leadership traits makes it easier to comprehend that leaders with divine masculine energy won't have a problem creating purpose-driven and compassionate environments conducive to growth and achievement.

Effective leadership is a dynamic concoction of qualities and traits beyond mere managerial skills.
https://pixabay.com/photos/mahatma-gandhi-india-independence-289158/

Traits of Successful Leaders

Physical Strength

In leadership roles, physical strength may not necessarily refer to literal physical prowess but rather to the resilience and endurance leaders exhibit in the face of challenges. It involves persevering through difficulties, maintaining stamina during demanding periods, and serving as a steadfast example.

Emotional Strength

Leadership often involves navigating complex and emotionally charged situations. Emotional strength is the ability to remain composed under pressure, handle criticism gracefully, and manage personal emotions effectively. Leaders with emotional strength are better equipped to make rational decisions, provide stability during turbulent times, and create a positive emotional climate around them.

Strategic Thinking

Successful leaders are distinguished by their strategic thinking abilities. That involves having a clear vision of the future and the capacity to devise comprehensive strategies to achieve long-term goals. Strategic thinking enables leaders to anticipate challenges, identify opportunities, and delegate purposefully toward a shared vision. It's a forward-looking mindset that aligns actions with overarching objectives, enabling organizational growth and sustainability.

Innovation

Visionary leaders are not only focused on existing goals but are also open to innovation. They encourage creativity within their teams, embracing new ideas and approaches to problem-solving. By practicing a culture of innovation, leaders ensure that their organizations remain dynamic and responsive to evolving challenges.

Decisiveness

Decisiveness is a fundamental aspect of effective leadership. Successful leaders make timely and well-informed decisions, even in the face of uncertainty. A decisive leader instills confidence in the team, maintains momentum, and ensures that opportunities are not missed. This quality is crucial for navigating complex situations, enabling leaders to take bold actions with clarity and purpose.

Accountability

Decision-making is accompanied by accountability in successful leadership. Leaders take responsibility for the outcomes of their decisions, whether positive or negative. This accountability promotes trust with everyone around. It also sets the stage for continuous improvement as leaders learn from successful outcomes and setbacks.

Honesty

Integrity is the bedrock of successful leadership, and honesty is a cornerstone of this quality. Leaders build trust by communicating transparently and authentically. Honest leaders are respected for their sincerity, and their actions align with their words. That creates a foundation of trust within the team and establishes the leader as a reliable and conscientious figure.

Consistency

Maintaining consistency in values and actions is integral to leadership integrity. Consistent leaders earn credibility by aligning their decisions and behaviors with a set of ethical principles. This consistency creates a sense of predictability and reliability, reinforcing followers' trust in their leader.

Openness to Feedback

Humble leaders actively seek and welcome feedback. They understand they don't have all the answers and are open to learning from others. This openness creates a culture of continuous improvement, where constructive criticism is seen as an opportunity for growth rather than a threat. By valuing the input of others, humble leaders foster a collaborative and inclusive work environment.

Understanding

Empathetic leaders demonstrate a deep understanding of their peers' needs, concerns, and perspectives. This understanding goes beyond surface-level interactions and involves actively listening to individuals, acknowledging their experiences, and considering their feelings. Leaders who cultivate empathy create a supportive work environment where everyone feels valued and understood.

Compassion

Beyond understanding, empathetic leaders express compassion for the well-being of their team members. Compassionate leaders create a sense of belonging and trust, as team members know their leader genuinely cares about their success and happiness.

Clarity

Leaders articulate their vision, expectations, and objectives in a manner easily understood by their team. Clear communication minimizes misunderstandings, aligns everyone towards common goals, and facilitates a cohesive and focused work environment.

Active Listening

Leaders who actively listen create an inclusive and collaborative culture. This two-way communication approach enhances problem-solving, innovation, and the team's overall well-being.

Risk-Taking

Courageous leaders are willing to take calculated risks in pursuit of organizational goals. Risk-taking drives innovation, explores new opportunities, and challenges the status quo.

Resilience

Resilient leaders bounce back from adversity, demonstrating a steadfast commitment to their vision and goals. Resilience boosts confidence in unfavorable times and sets the tone for a positive and determined organizational culture.

Examining these qualities and traits in detail gives you a clear picture of the multifaceted nature of successful leadership. These attributes are not isolated. Instead, they interact and complement each other, shaping leaders who can navigate complexities, inspire people around them, and contribute to holistic growth.

Exploring Divine Masculine Leadership

Leadership roles inspired by the divine masculine energy require a solid integration of strength, vision, and compassion. Drawing inspiration from this energy, you can embody a leadership style that transcends conventional paradigms. The divine masculine principles guide leaders toward a balanced expression of power, purpose, and empathy. It involves recognizing the inherent strength in vulnerability, the vision in compassion, and the power in humility. Leaders attuned to the divine masculine principles become facilitators of growth, creating and supporting environments where both individual and collective potential blooms.

Transformational Leadership

Transformational leadership aligns closely with the principles of the divine masculine. This leadership style follows transactional exchanges and aims to inspire and elevate followers toward higher performance levels. Furthermore, leaders with transformational leadership promote a sense of purpose and vision, emphasizing collective goals over individual pursuits. They act as role models, showcasing the strength and resilience associated with the divine masculine while fostering empathy and compassion.

Within the divine masculine framework, transformational leaders leverage strength to inspire change, vision to guide transformation, and empathy to connect with and understand the needs of their team. Transformational leadership is an excellent example of harmonious synergy between the elements of divine masculine energy and effective leadership.

Servant Leadership

Servant leadership, rooted in the idea of leaders serving their teams, resonates strongly with divine masculine principles. Leaders embracing this style prioritize the well-being and growth of their team members with humility and empathy. Servant leaders recognize that true strength lies in empowering others, and true vision encompasses a collective journey toward success.

A servant leader draws strength from their ability to support, guide, and uplift others. This leadership style aligns with the concept of the divine masculine as a force that nurtures and protects, creating a balanced and inclusive environment where everyone feels valued.

Creating a Balance

Leaders aspiring to embody the divine masculine principles must strike a balance between strength, vision, and compassion. Strength in this context is about being resilient when facing challenges and steadfast in achieving a shared vision. Likewise, the vision leaders will set goals and inspire others to see and believe in the larger purpose. Compassion, rooted in empathy, is the glue that will bind the team together, promoting trust and collaboration.

Leaders who successfully integrate these elements create a dynamic and supportive organizational culture. They recognize that the divine masculine is not about dominance but about harmonizing power and compassion, strength and vulnerability, and vision and empathy. Leaders with this mindset can become catalysts for positive change, shaping environments where individuals can thrive, contribute meaningfully, and collectively achieve their highest potential.

Leadership as a Divine Masculine

The emphasis here is not on asserting dominance or control but on empowering others to rise and shine. The divine masculine leader operates from a position of strength, not to overpower others but to provide the necessary support and guidance, helping their peers and subordinates reach their full potential. Here are key aspects of how the divine masculine leader empowers others:

Supportive Guidance

Instead of micromanaging or imposing control, the divine masculine leader offers supportive guidance. This involves providing a framework for growth and success, allowing individuals the autonomy to navigate their path while offering assistance and wisdom when needed. The leader acts as a mentor and ally, creating an environment where each team member feels encouraged to explore their capabilities.

Fostering Collaboration

Instead of enforcing a hierarchical structure, the divine masculine leader promotes collaboration. The focus is on building a collective vision where each person's contributions are valued. This collaborative approach harnesses the diverse talents within the team.

Nurturing Potential

Divine masculine leadership is committed to nurturing the potential within each individual. Leaders focus on understanding team members' unique talents and aspirations and work towards creating opportunities for them to shine. This approach inspires a sense of purpose and fulfillment, as team members are encouraged to express their full potential within the organizational context.

Cultivating a Growth Mindset

Divine masculine leadership promotes a growth mindset within the team. Instead of focusing on fixed roles or limitations, the leader encourages a mindset of continuous learning and improvement. This perspective creates a culture where individuals realize their evolving potential and harness the courage to face challenges.

Case Studies

While it's challenging to definitively attribute success to the embodiment of specific divine masculine qualities, some leaders exhibit characteristics aligned with the principles of strength, vision, compassion, and empowerment. Here are a few examples:

Nelson Mandela

Divine Masculine Qualities: Strength, Vision, Empowerment

The former President of South Africa, Nelson Mandela, exemplified the divine masculine qualities of strength and resilience during his long imprisonment. His unwavering commitment to the vision of a united and democratic South Africa, despite immense personal sacrifice, showcased visionary leadership. After his release, Mandela focused on the divine masculine abilities of reconciliation and empowerment, promoting unity and steering the nation towards a new era.

Mahatma Gandhi
Divine Masculine Qualities: Vision, Compassion, Empowerment

Mahatma Gandhi was a famous leader of India's non-violent independence movement who portrayed divine masculine qualities of compassion and empowerment. His vision for a free and united India inspired millions to join the struggle for independence. Gandhi's leadership was fueled by a profound empathy for the oppressed and a commitment to non-violent resistance.

Martin Luther King Jr.
Divine Masculine Qualities: Vision, Empowerment, Strength

Martin Luther King Jr. was a prominent leader in the American civil rights movement with divine masculine qualities, advocated for equality, and showed strength in the face of adversity. His famous "I Have a Dream" speech articulated a vision of a racially integrated and harmonious America. King's leadership strengthened marginalized communities, contributing to significant societal changes and inspiring future leaders globally.

Elon Musk
Divine Masculine Qualities: Vision, Innovation

Elon Musk, CEO of SpaceX and Tesla, exemplifies divine masculine qualities through his visionary approach to technology and innovation. His bold vision of colonizing Mars with SpaceX and transforming the automotive industry with Tesla demonstrates a commitment to transformative goals. His leadership style empowers his teams to pursue ambitious projects, promoting a culture of innovation and pushing the boundaries of what is possible.

Oprah Winfrey
Divine Masculine Qualities: Compassion, Empowerment, Vision

She is a well-known media personality and philanthropist with divine masculine compassion and empowering leadership qualities. Her inspiring and uplifting energy for media has shaped her successful career. Winfrey's leadership extends beyond her media empire, as she has used her influence to kickstart initiatives promoting education, health, and personal development.

These examples illustrate that leaders who practice divine masculine qualities can profoundly impact organizations, communities, and society at large. Whether through political change, social justice movements, technological advancements, or media influence, these leaders demonstrate how strength, vision, compassion, and empowerment can contribute to positive and transformative leadership outcomes.

Emotional Intelligence in Leadership with Divine Masculine Qualities

Emotional intelligence is crucial to effective leadership, enhancing interpersonal relationships, decision-making, and overall organizational success. Emotional intelligence creates a powerful leadership paradigm when combined with divine masculine qualities like strength, vision, and empowerment. Here's how self-regulation, empathy, and motivation work together to cultivate divine masculine qualities in a leader.

Self-Regulation

Self-regulation within the divine masculine context involves maintaining composure, resilience, and steadiness in the face of challenges. A leader with divine masculine qualities employs self-regulation to channel strength into constructive actions, avoiding impulsive reactions.

Tips and Techniques

- **Mindfulness Practices**: Engage in mindfulness meditation to cultivate self-awareness and control over emotional responses.
- **Reflective Journaling**: Regularly journaling emotions and reactions helps develop awareness and fosters self-regulation.
- **Breathing Exercises**: Deep breathing exercises can effectively manage stress and promote emotional balance.

Empathy

Empathy in the divine masculine leadership context is about understanding the needs and concerns of others while maintaining strength and support. A leader with divine masculine qualities uses empathy to connect with team members and promote a collaborative and supportive environment.

Tips and Techniques
- **Active Listening**: Practice attentive and empathetic listening to fully understand others' perspectives.
- **Seeking Feedback**: Actively seek feedback from team members to understand their experiences and viewpoints.
- **Put Yourself in Others' Shoes**: Develop the habit of considering situations from others' perspectives to enhance empathetic understanding.

Motivation

In the divine masculine leadership framework, motivation involves inspiring others toward a shared vision. A leader with divine masculine qualities leverages motivation to energize the team, aligning their efforts with a higher purpose.

Tips and Techniques
- **Clarify Personal Values**: Align personal values with organizational goals to fuel intrinsic motivation.
- **Set Inspiring Goals**: Establish challenging yet achievable goals that resonate with the team's sense of purpose.
- **Celebrate Achievements**: Acknowledge and celebrate individual and team accomplishments to sustain motivation.

Integration of Traits

Emotionally intelligent leaders with divine masculine qualities strike a balance between strength and sensitivity. They use their strength to provide support and empowerment, while their emotional intelligence enables them to navigate complex interpersonal dynamics with empathy and understanding. These leaders combine their visionary mindset with empathy, ensuring that their strategic decisions consider the well-being and perspectives of their team members. They communicate the larger vision in a way that resonates emotionally, inspiring commitment and collaboration.

Challenges and Growth

A leader with divine masculine qualities and high emotional intelligence recognizes the strength in vulnerability. They acknowledge their own emotions and vulnerabilities, creating an authentic connection with their team. Achieving and maintaining emotional intelligence is an ongoing process. Leaders with divine masculine qualities are committed to continuous self-reflection, learning, and growth, recognizing that emotional intelligence is a dynamic skill that evolves over time.

Effective Communication Strategies

Clarity in Expression

Effective communication begins with clarity in expression, a fundamental trait of divine masculine leadership. Leaders in this paradigm value straightforward messaging, aiming to convey information clearly and directly. This approach reduces the likelihood of misunderstandings and ensures that the entire team shares a common understanding of organizational goals. Leaders often use concrete examples to illustrate points to achieve this clarity, making communication more tangible and accessible to team members.

Assertiveness with Respect

Divine masculine leaders communicate with a unique blend of confidence and respect. Assertiveness is key to their communication style, inspiring trust and decisiveness. However, this assertiveness is balanced with a commitment to active listening, demonstrating genuine interest in others' perspectives.

Alignment with Vision

Alignment with the overarching vision is a critical dimension of divine masculine communication. Leaders ensure that every message, whether conveyed in team meetings or written communications, is consistent with the larger purpose and goals of the organization. This consistency reinforces the shared vision and enhances the team's commitment to it. Also, leaders actively connect day-to-day actions to the overarching vision, clarifying how specific tasks contribute to the realization of shared organizational goals.

Openness to Dialogue

Openness to dialogue is a hallmark of divine masculine communication. Leaders encourage open and constructive dialogue within the team. Addressing challenges directly and constructively is prioritized, as divine masculine leaders understand that facing conflicts head-on contributes to the overall strength and resilience of the team.

Empowering Language

Empowering language is a key aspect of divine masculine communication. Leaders use inclusive pronouns and avoid language that may create a sense of hierarchy or exclusion. Instead, they choose pronouns that emphasize collective ownership and shared responsibility. Regularly acknowledging and appreciating the contributions of team members is a standard practice.

Adaptability in Communication

Adaptability in communication is also emphasized within the divine masculine leadership approach. Leaders recognize that different individuals may respond to communication styles differently. They tailor their approach to suit the needs and preferences of various team members. Establishing feedback loops is essential to ensure that communication remains effective, with ongoing encouragement for team members to provide feedback on communication processes.

Inspiring through Storytelling

Inspiring through storytelling is a powerful divine masculine communication strategy. Leaders craft compelling narratives illustrating the journey, challenges, and triumphs aligned with the shared vision. Storytelling engages emotions, making the message more memorable and inspiring for the team. When appropriate, connecting on a human level by sharing personal stories and experiences humanizes leadership and builds trust.

Setting Expectations

Setting expectations is integral to divine masculine communication. Leaders set clear expectations for their team, communicating roles, responsibilities, and goals with transparency. This clarity prevents misunderstandings and ensures everyone is aligned with the vision and purpose. Regular updates on progress toward goals reinforce the connection between individual efforts and the larger vision.

Incorporating these communication strategies enhances divine masculine qualities in leadership and contributes to the overall effectiveness of communication, fostering a positive and empowered organizational culture.

Chapter 7: Enhancing the Connection: Meditation

The divine masculine is always functioning inside of you. However, there may be interference with the connection, like the static you hear when the signal is bad on the phone. Much like when you want to get a stronger connection on a phone call, you need to shift your position to hear the sacred masculine more clearly. Unlike with the phone, this movement does not happen in the physical, but it occurs in the mind. Meditation is the pathway to shifting the position of the mind.

Meditation is the pathway to shifting the position of the mind.
https://www.pexels.com/photo/man-wearing-black-cap-with-eyes-closed-under-cloudy-sky-810775/

Mindfulness practices and meditation bring you into the present moment. The divine masculine does not function in the past or future. It only exists in the now. The barrier to connecting with the sacred masculine is overthinking about the past and future. When you dwell on moments that no longer exist or don't yet exist, it takes away from the action you can take now. Therefore, the doorway to manifesting the divine masculine is the use of meditation, mindfulness, grounding, and affirmations to put you in the position to move forward from the trap of your mind.

Understanding Meditation and Mindfulness as the Gateway to the Divine Masculine

Meditation is a vehicle to navigate yourself. Like with any other vehicle, it takes some practice before you can fully control it. A defining attribute of the sacred masculine is that it embodies pinpoint accuracy. Thoughts and perceptions are the distortions that decenter people, throwing them off from an accurate view of reality. Meditation allows you to realize you are not your thoughts and perceptions. Identifying with the observer of your thoughts instead of the thoughts themselves enables you to control and direct your thinking with complete autonomy. Before you can righteously rule over any aspect of your life by functioning within your divine masculinity, you need to control yourself. Meditation helps you understand your true self to mold what emanates from you alchemically.

Meditation dissociates you from your thoughts, worries, biases, and perceptions so you can align with the person within who is beyond these concepts. When you identify with the distortions of what you believe you are, you are empowered to step into knowing. The divine masculine demands a precise, logical, and constant reassessment of how you function within society. Meditation slows you down to allow you to separate from your functionality and tap into a pure sense of existence. From the foundation of existence, you can start to craft the life you want by ordering your thoughts.

Reality begins in the mind. Think of thoughts as a low-density expression of existence. For thoughts to manifest into the external world, they get filtered through higher densities to become tangible. The abstract reality of your thoughts represents the dark feminine because they are hidden from the world in the womb. The masculine plants the seed of action to bring these thoughts into reality. The unbalanced masculine will bring chaos and destruction, while the aligned masculine will create a disciplined order that benefits you and the community. To align your masculine expression, you go inward to the observer of your thoughts to assess what is worthy of taking action. That is how meditation provides the clarity needed to enhance the divine masculine.

Mindfulness is bringing yourself into the present moment. Meditation techniques can enhance your mindfulness. In the present, you are more in tune with what is tangible because the past and the future exist only in your imagination. Remember, the divine masculine is not about the abstract but what is more solid. Condensing your thoughts and desires into reality through the filter of masculinity first requires a profound understanding of the intricacies of what you think. Mindfully being present lets you see which thoughts are relevant to your current situation and which ones will better you right now. This presentness equips you to manipulate your steps according to the reality you want to manifest.

Meditation and mindfulness put you in a better position to make clear and sober decisions, free from the filters of perception and biases. When you meditate, you realize that you may not control what you think, but you have supreme control over how to respond to your thoughts. An ill-disciplined person who has not matured into their divine masculinity becomes a victim to their thoughts, often taking irrational action that can lead to disastrous consequences like ending up in toxic relationships and, in extreme cases, even taking a trip to prison. Meditation and mindfulness are the hammer and chisel that allow you to carve your path out of the material of your thoughts and perceptions.

Anchoring Yourself to Clarity and Strength with Breathing

Breath is one of the most powerful tools for accessing the portal of meditation and mindfulness to the divine masculine. Humans can go without food for a few weeks and a few days without water. However, you can only go without breath for a couple of minutes. Breath is one of the most potent living energies a human has access to. Breathing is a harmonizing force within your system. Your breathing patterns change according to your physical, psychological, and emotional condition. For example, when you are angry or anxious, your breathing will speed up, and when you are calm, it slows down.

In the Biblical narrative, breath is equated to life because it was when God breathed into man's nostrils that he became a living being. The Hebrew word ruach can be used to describe both spirit and breath. In the Hindu tradition, prana is a life force energy that flows through all things, including human bodies. To manage this pranic energy, you must control your breath. Breath is deeply tied to all forms of spirituality across multiple practices. You can find a linguistic link between spirituality and respiration through the letter "spir" as in SPIRit, or reSPIRation. Your breathing and mental state are intrinsically linked.

In meditation, breath control is one of the simplest ways to promote focus and clarity. The beauty of the breath is that it operates automatically, but when you decide to, you can consciously take control of your breathing. Breath control, especially during meditation, is how you can exercise your focus muscle to bring clarity. The technique of breath control can also contribute to gaining both mental and physical strength. For example, professional fighters learn to control their breath under immense strain to maintain energy throughout their match.

Breath control can start with a simple mindfulness meditation exercise. Sit down in a comfortable position with your eyes closed. Allow yourself to breathe as you normally would for a few minutes while you let all your thoughts drift in and out. Do this until you realize your thoughts are beginning to loop, and the same ideas are re-emerging. Now, start controlling the pace of your breathing by bringing your attention to it. Breathe in for five seconds through your nose, and then exhale out of your mouth for five seconds. Whenever your mind wanders, bring your attention back to your breath. When you inhale, focus on how the breath feels entering your nostrils and how your stomach expands. Then, when you exhale, focus on your breath leaving your mouth and how your stomach compresses. That will bring calmness, releasing all the stress from your body and allowing you to gain mental clarity. Furthermore, it creates a body and mind unity needed to engage with the divine masculine.

Stability is one of the central pillars of the sacred masculine. You cannot be stable when you are in a heightened and anxious state. People cannot rely on you as a masculine support if emotions and frantic thoughts easily sway you. Breathing is the key that unlocks a divine emotional control that releases you from stress and anxiety so that you can function in the calm stoicism of masculinity in the face of all kinds of adversities. The world will throw curveballs at you, but you can knock them out of the park by focusing through breath control. A few minutes of conscious breathing before you decide or take action could be the difference between success and failure.

Grounding Yourself

Everything in creation is based on balance. Depending on how you view the earth, it can be personified as masculine or feminine. For example, in Greek mythology, Gaia is the earth goddess, while in Egyptian mythology, the earth is personified as masculine through the god Geb. One of the feminine aspects of the earth is the soil, which gives rise to all the plants and trees. Looking at it through the sacred masculine lens, the mountains and rocks represent a stable and strong masculine essence. Therefore, you access the energy of strength and stability when you use grounding.

Grounding is the practice of using your body to connect with the earth's electricity. Using grounding techniques like walking barefoot on natural ground has numerous physical and psychological benefits. Grounding reduces inflammation in the body, which leads to pain relief and accelerated healing. It also helps you sleep better, which has the psychological benefits of stress reduction, improved mood, and increased focus at work or in your studies. Grounding is one of the simplest activities to connect with the sacred masculine. All you need to do is stand barefoot on soil or grass.

Grounding can be combined with meditation and mindfulness. Envisioning roots sprawling from your feet as you stand on soil or grass establishes a mental connection with the earth in addition to the physical one that your feet touching the ground create. When your roots spread deeply into the earth, reflect on how stabilizing the energy they pull up into your body is. Meditating on the idea of rooting into physical reality is the mental fuel you need to chase down your desires by working on them diligently.

Everybody wears shoes with rubber, plastic, or foam soles in the modern era. This disconnects people from the electricity flowing through the earth. Electricity is like the masculine form of energy, while magnetism represents the feminine. Therefore, humans are electromagnetic beings. The magnetism within you is to attract, while the electricity presents the giving power. Just like the electricity on appliances is used to bring them to life, when grounding, the energy absorbed through the conductors of your feet is rejuvenating and revitalizing.

The central spiritual benefit of grounding is that it reintroduces you to the planet. Many have been misled through modern systems to believe that mankind owns the earth. This misinformation is done through many blatant and subtle programs. For example, people buy and sell land and trade the produce that the earth provides. In reality, the earth owns you. It is your metaphorical mother. Everything your body is comprised of comes from the planet, and when you die, it will get recycled into other living and non-living things. The Bible writes about how humanity came from dust and how you'll return to dust in death. Similarly, the Holy Quran mentions how Adam was made from mud. The grounding connects you to a primal reality that has long been forgotten due to the distortions of modernity.

Not only does grounding connect you with the planet, but it also connects you to all living beings that call Earth home. The surface you stand on can be followed around the world to any random place on the planet through the connections of organic material. Grounding aligns you with nature and your fellow humans while reestablishing a primordial connection with yourself.

Trust and Receptivity Through Crafting a Tranquil Spiritual Space

Transformation starts on the inside. That is not where it stops, however. Your space reflects your internal being. The inner transformation is the foundation, but what is around you can help cultivate that transformative energy. All faith traditions worldwide have some form of elaborate temple because of the universal understanding that the human vehicles of perception, or the senses, are portals. What you consume will eventually influence you. If you constantly eat junk food, after some time, you'll become overweight. Your mouth is not the only portal into your body. Your eyes, ears, and nose also consume whatever is around you. Having a tranquil meditation and mindfulness space to retreat to as a refilling station can be exceedingly helpful.

Practicing in a space fine-tuned to your personal expression of spirituality makes you more receptive to the divine masculinity and trusting to the changes harnessing this potent energy. The subconscious mind does not speak English or any other language but rather communicates in signs and symbols. Only you can craft a space that promotes the mythos you want to unfold in your life. The symbology embedded into your tranquil sanctuary must make sense to your journey because symbols are not always universal. For example, a baseball bat will mean something different to a gangster who uses it to attack people than someone who plays baseball with their grandfather whom they love dearly. Introspect on the masculine attributes like discipline, strength, clarity, and focus, which you would like to grow in your personality. Now, what symbolizes these attributes in your life? You may be a wrestling fan, so Hulk Hogan could symbolize the height of strength, so you can include a poster of him in your space.

Think of the predominant energies you are attempting to manifest and direct your meditation space in that direction. Use all your senses, like smell, sight, and sound. You may want to include a speaker to play calming, meditative music or incorporate pleasant-smelling incense into the room. If you are religious, you can include the icons of your faith. You can also incorporate drums or sound bowls or even decorate the space with pictures of your loved ones. Some people find vision boards useful, so you can fill the room with pictures of the life you want to live or the goals you want to achieve.

The meditation and mindfulness practices you embrace should also be considered when creating your tranquil space. You know yourself better than anybody else. A mission needs to be completed in this room, namely practicing meditative practices to make you receptive and trusting of the divine masculine. This room is not a "mancave" created for pleasure-seeking and escapism. It is a space dedicated to transformative spiritual practice, so minimize distractions and maximize what puts you on the path to opening up yourself for the sacred masculine to come through.

Don't do anything else in your created space other than your spiritual practices. For example, avoid having social visits in the space or finishing up work there. Assign those tasks to other more appropriate areas. It would be inappropriate for someone to throw a rave in a temple because it is dedicated to devotion to God. Similarly, you must respect your spiritual space and set up strong boundaries for yourself and others. Taking some time out of your day to specifically focus on stoking the internal sacred masculine flames can be greatly enhanced when you have an area to go to dedicated to that goal.

Affirmations to Awaken the Sacred Masculine

Affirmations are like mantras or positive statements you repeat to yourself every day so that you can embody what you are saying with your actions. Your speech is the next level of reality that is a step away from your thoughts. Speaking is the beginning of creation. The Genesis account in the Bible says that God spoke the world into existence. This is linked to the third Hermetic principle, which is vibration. Everything is constantly in motion or vibrates at various frequencies. Your speech is a vibration as well, so it has an impact on the physical world. Hearing your voice confirm positive statements influences your mind to take action to live out the statements you make in your affirmations.

Furthermore, the "I am" before most affirmations is a magical statement. When Moses asked God in the Bible what His name was, God replied, "I am that I am." Saying "I am" brings reality to the present moment. It is not the wishful thinking of statements like "I want to be," but rather, it embraces existence in your current space and time. Affirming through the pathway of "I am" recalibrates your mind to accept the statement as true because everything begins in the mental space before it becomes apparent externally. Affirmations are meant to put you in the mentality where you already embody the qualities of the divine masculine instead of hoping one day to achieve them like some sort of distant apparition.

Here is a list of affirmations that are specifically created to assist you in connecting with your divine masculinity more deeply:

- I am a warrior.
- I am confident.
- I know when to take action.
- I am strong.
- I am dedicated to my vision.
- I am disciplined.
- I am patient.
- I am a stable pillar of my home and community.
- I am reliable.
- I am honest and straightforward.
- I am brave.

- I am courageous.
- I overcome all obstacles.
- I am present.
- I am aware.
- I am focused.
- I am resilient and persevere through all hardships.
- I am immovable.
- I am solid.
- I am a powerful leader.
- I am whole.
- I embody the divine masculine in its highest capacity.

You don't have to use all these affirmations. Pick five to ten that most closely resonate with who you are and what you want to achieve. You could also use the list as is if you feel so inclined. Writing your own affirmations specifically catering to your situation is also helpful. Remember to begin the statement with "I am," followed by a positive and affirming sentence. Repeat your affirmation five times in the morning and five times in the evening. It is best to say your affirmations in front of a mirror. Seeing yourself makes them more impactful.

Chapter 8: Finding the Balance Within

Divine Union of Masculine and Feminine

The common view of marriage in the Western world is that two people leave their parents and commit to one another to become one unit. If you break this down mathematically, it can be conceptualized as $1 + 0 = 1$. In this numerological representation of the divine union of feminine and masculine, the male is represented by 1, and the female is represented by 0. When you compare these numbers to biology, you find that 1 has a phallic shape representing the male sexual organ while the round shape of 0 represents the womb. When the two come together, they are equal to one, meaning there is no separation or duality. Biologically and mythologically, this is presented as the Mother and Father bringing forth the Child.

Internally, the divine union is when the feminine and masculine aspects of yourself are balanced.
https://www.pexels.com/photo/closeup-photography-of-stacked-stones-1051449/

Therefore, to manifest anything, you need both the masculine and feminine to be present. If you look at the marriage tradition of exchanging rings, you find the external mirror of the divine union. The ring is placed on the finger to symbolize the bond and commitment of the couple to act in one another's best interest. The finger could be interpreted as male, while the ring is female. The finger and the ring make contact to seal the bond of masculine and feminine commitment.

Internally, the divine union is when the feminine and masculine aspects of yourself are balanced. The simplest way to understand this is by viewing the feminine as chaos and the masculine as order. When there is too much chaos in a society, you get lawless anarchy; when there is too much order, you get authoritative tyranny. Both of these outcomes result in death and destruction. Therefore, to function as a whole actualized human, you need to embrace the divine feminine and the divine masculine.

An egg is an analogy of how the divine feminine and masculine balance should work. The shell is masculine, while the internal contents of the egg are feminine. The important part of the egg that turns into a chicken is on the inside. However, the chicken cannot come into existence without the hard shell of masculine protection. In some ways, the vulnerable and emotional parts of yourself are the most real representations of your being, but to function in society, they must be housed in the divine masculine. The purpose of the divine masculine is to deliver the sacred feminine into the world in a way where it can be accepted and protected. In a practical sense, this means allowing yourself to be vulnerable, emotional, and expressive while setting protective boundaries for the world not to take advantage of you.

The divine masculine is like a container, and the sacred feminine is like water. The water flows according to where the container guides it. Therefore, masculinity is often related to leadership. However, to lead, there must be goals, so sometimes, the feminine water shapes the masculine container like a river carving a mountain into a particular shape. This interplay of the water carving up the land, but the land also guiding the water, is what the union of feminine and masculine looks like. Neither is less or more important, but both are needed for you to exist healthily.

Symbolic Representations of Masculine and Feminine Balance in Philosophy and Mythology

The divine feminine and masculine have been symbolized throughout the ages through mythical figures, deities, and philosophical concepts. The idea is so fundamental to existence that it has been presented across cultures and time in an array of forms. In the Hindu pantheon, Shiva and Shakti have personified masculine and feminine energy. The feminine took the form of Parvati and Kali, both representations of Shakti, while the masculine came forth as Shiva.

One of the central narratives to understand the relationship between the divine feminine and masculine is how Kali defeats the demon hoards led by Raktabija, who terrorizes other gods and sages. Kali easily defeated the demons, drinking their blood and beheading them. However, the volatile Shakti energy got so out of control that it became terrifying and dangerous. Lord Shiva went to calm her down. In her uncontrollable rage, she killed him, throwing him to the ground. Once she realized what she had done, she calmed down to breathe life back into Shiva.

This narrative highlights how the creative and powerfully feminine energy gets channeled through the masculine so that it can become ordered. Another way to think of this is as a child who has not yet been socialized. They will hit and bite others and have chaotic emotional outbursts. Over time, they get socialized and begin learning which behaviors are appropriate. If an adult were to behave in the same unhinged manner as a child, it would cause massive disorder with disastrous consequences. A child gets taught how to channel their emotions and communicate their displeasure in more cooperative ways. So, Shakti, as Kali, would be the raw emotional expression of the child, while Shiva is the order that comes through when the emotions are constrained to various pathways.

The universe is made out of matter and energy. Matter can be framed as the masculine, while energy is the feminine. This gendered view of reality permeates all aspects of life. It is then essential to understand that divine feminine and sacred masculine don't necessarily refer to man and woman. When this energy is looked at through such a narrow lens, it lends itself to becoming offensive or even exploitative. Using the words feminine and masculine are just ways to personify concepts to make them easier to understand. In the beginning, the universe existed in a raw state of energy. After the Big Bang, or the masculine seed, was planted, matter developed as an ordered way to express this energy. This is how Shakti and Shiva work together.

Yin and yang is another great example of the divine masculine and sacred feminine described in an ancient culture. Yin is the dark, negative, contemplative, passive, and feminine. Don't think of negative in a moral sense, but rather like the negative charge on a battery or the negative numbers in mathematics. Yang is more active, positive, and masculine. Yin and yang originate from the ancient Chinese Daoist tradition, highlighting how opposing forces create reality to achieve a union of all. To become whole, the Daoist tradition requires a deep understanding of balance, which its practices and philosophies emphasize.

Carl Jung had a unique perspective on the masculine and feminine because he viewed them through the psychological lens. Jung developed the concept of the anima and the animus. Generally, the persona of a man presents as masculine, and that of a woman presents as feminine. The persona is the mask you wear to fit into society. This masculine or feminine persona needs to be balanced to create an internal projection of the ideal man or woman. This ideal is called the animus for women and the anima for men. When a man has integrated his anima, he will healthily express his emotions without being overly domineering. When a woman has integrated her animus, she will be logical, problem-solving, and driven. The anima can then be seen as the feminine aspect of a man, and the animus can be viewed as the male aspect of a woman. To be a whole person, you must integrate this internal part of yourself so you can express both masculine and feminine characteristics appropriately.

What Is the Divine Feminine?

Without understanding the divine feminine, you'll never be able to grasp the concept of the sacred masculine because these two personifications of energy and matter are two sides of the same coin. The feminine and masculine exist on the same spectrum. To analyze one, you need the other. You cannot understand what hot is unless you have experienced cold before to compare it to. If the temperature constantly stayed the same, there would be no hot or cold. Similarly, the masculine and feminine can only be understood due to their juxtaposition. To unlock your divine masculine to its fullest expression, you must also work on the divine feminine.

Where masculine energy is driven, logical, active, giving, and orderly, feminine energy is the exact opposite: emotional, irrational, passive, receiving, and chaotic. The divine feminine is the nurturing softness and vulnerability needed to maintain healthy relationships. It can also be described as the abstract, the mental, and the internal. You need reason and emotion to be balanced in your sacred feminine and masculine. Human beings are not robots, so they cannot function in a sterile state devoid of passion. The divine feminine submits while the sacred masculine leads. However, the feminine also guides. If you use the analogy of a housewife and a working husband, the wife tells the husband everything needed or desired to make the home functional and warm, and then the husband goes out to work to get all those things. So, the divine feminine are your dreams, visions, and passions expressed through physical actions in the sacred masculine space.

Your dreams can be chaotic. Think about your past dreams. Dream sequences don't function rationally. The sequences are not always linear, and the physics of the dream often does not make sense. However, when you are in that realm, the way it functions is not jarring, but it seems normal until you wake up and realize how odd it is. Dreams are where the subconscious mind rationalizes and analyzes your well-being and different events that have occurred recently or in the past. In the chaos of a dream, deep truths are revealed. To integrate these truths and take action accordingly, you can institute the logical masculine to dissect the dream into parts and gain valuable insight to apply in your waking life.

The divine feminine is loving, caring, and nurturing, but at the same time can be volatile and vindictive. When feminine energy is imbalanced, it can result in instability, poisoned relationships, and deceptive manipulation. The story of Medusa best describes how the divine feminine can get so distorted. Medusa was cursed as a result of an illicit affair with the sea god, Poseidon. Her hair was turned to snakes, and any man who looked at her was turned to stone. Men transforming to stone by looking at her is a symbolic representation of masculine arousal. By getting poisoned by fake love, Medusa is no longer able to maintain relationships, instead taking a monstrous form that breaks all the men she comes into contact with through lustful desire. Symbolically, this can be interpreted as someone who has experienced hardships and trauma, becoming bitter and unable to embody the soft feminine. Their value becomes tied to how they can be used and how they can use others. The healthy feminine vulnerability is destroyed by trauma.

The divine feminine also represents spiritual cleansing. The internal work you require to heal from past traumas gets messy. Therefore, only the feminine chaotic energy can be used to heal you. You cannot reason your way out of the unreasonable hurt you've experienced. You need to feel it fully without any logical justifications. Then, you bring in the masculine energy of order to see how deeply ingrained experiences can be integrated into your psyche to produce positive outcomes. The first step, though, is opening the door to flush out the dirt and grime of the past.

Case Study of Harmonizing the Masculine and Feminine: The Story of Mike Tyson

One of the best examples of balanced masculine and feminine energy is the story of Mike Tyson, one of the most legendary boxers to ever put on gloves. Very few people don't know the name of Iron Mike Tyson. His impact has been felt beyond the ring, making him a household name even among people who are not boxing fans. Today, Mike Tyson has a podcast called "Hotboxin' with Mike Tyson," and many see him as a wise sage due to his enlightening and introspective advice.

Tyson's early life was filled with turmoil as his drug-addicted mother sold her body to support the family and her habit. Both Tyson's father and stepfather abandoned the family when he was young. He grew up in Brownsville, a dangerous area of New York that was riddled with crime and poverty. He fell into the dangerous lifestyle of crime and violence that many in his neighborhood embraced before finding an outlet in boxing. His coach, Cus D'Amato, trained Tyson to be an emotionless assassin, which led him to become a world champion.

Today's kind, gentle, but still scary Mike Tyson is far from who he was at the height of his career. He still holds the record for most first-round and second-round knockouts in boxing history. His ferocious peek-a-boo style and terrifying power demolished all opponents who dared to step in front of him, making him the youngest heavyweight champion in the world at the age of 19. His career spiraled out of control after the death of his father figure, coach, and mentor, Cus D'Amato. His excessive partying, drug addiction, and violent lifestyle eventually led him to prison.

When Tyson came back from prison, he was not immediately reformed. However, he eventually reached a crossroads where he realized that he needed to make a change and address the young, scared, and abused boy who still lived inside of him. Through dedicated effort and spiritual practice, Tyson was able to get in touch with his softer side, evolving into the wise and gentle man many know him as today.

Tyson is a living representation of the balance between masculine and feminine. He loved Cus D'Amato and often burst into tears when talking about him. However, D'Amato trained Tyson to be a savage, and the love he had for him was based on the condition that Tyson stayed committed to becoming the best fighter in the world. This transactional form of love and stoking the flames of measured masculinity resulted in Tyson's underdeveloped emotional side. Tyson never dealt with the trauma of his early life, so he looked for an escape through drugs and violence. It was only when Tyson awakened the inner feminine side to become more loving and nurturing to the abused little boy inside of him that he was able to become whole enough to have a healthier expression of masculinity. He had to give himself the feminine love he had never received from his parents, community, or even from his beloved mentor, Cus. In finding this love through psychological and spiritual work, Tyson could balance the masculine and feminine, meaning that he could do excruciating damage but had the introspective self-control to act lovingly.

Mindfulness and Self-Awareness to Detect Imbalances in Yourself

Much like Tyson had to recognize that the scared little boy inside of him is what led him to express himself violently, you need to analyze yourself to identify which imbalances you have. The first step is blatant honesty. People tend to tell themselves lies so they can meaningfully exist in the world without facing their inner demons, which manifest in most of the problems in their lives. There is always this dynamic of the blame game and pointing fingers at the external world about why things are not going the way you would like them to. If you search within yourself, you'll find why you keep repeating many of the same mistakes and get attracted to negative relationships that bring you down.

Write down the answers to the following questions. Remember to be as honest as possible so that the exercise can reveal some of the deeper truths you keep buried and hidden.

1. What are the three main issues that you see constantly manifesting in my life?
2. What limitations or flaws in yourself have caused these issues?
3. Write down a scenario from the past where these flaws have resulted in a negative outcome.
4. How could the outcome have been worse?
5. How could the outcome have been better?
6. What should you change about yourself to prevent this flaw from continually hindering you?
7. What are your weaknesses?
8. How have your weaknesses held you back?
9. How can you minimize the negative impact of your weaknesses?
10. What are the origins of your weaknesses in childhood?
11. What are your strengths?
12. How have your strengths benefitted you?
13. What are the origins of your strengths in childhood?

Answering these questions will make you more self-aware and point you in the right direction of applying the healing and nurturing divine feminine, as well as the sacred masculine actions you can take to grow and improve yourself.

The following mindfulness visualization exercise will help you balance your masculine and feminine. The exercise will help heal your inner child and equip you with the tools to move forward and make informed decisions about your life.

Start by lying down and taking a few deep breaths in and out.

Imagine yourself in the middle of a cold and windy desert.

In the desert, you find a deep black hole that you cannot see the bottom of.

You notice an old wooden ladder at the edge of the hole.

Begin climbing down the ladder to the bottom of the hole. There is no light inside the hole, and it is completely dark. You cannot see anything, but you hear the faint echoes of a child crying.

As you descend, the crying gets louder.

Eventually, you reach the bottom of the hole, where you find a child crying, curled up in a ball.

You approach the child, who is still a shadowy outline in the darkness. When you get close enough to see the child, his back is turned towards you. You tap the child on the shoulder and find it was you when you were ten.

Ask the child why they are crying.

What did they say?

You give the child a big, loving hug to ease their pain.

The child lets out a joyful giggle.

Now, ask the child what you should do when you get back to your world at the top of the hole.

Slowly climb up the ladder as the child joyfully waves goodbye, thanking you for your help.

As you get closer to the top of the hole while climbing, you see light breaking through.

When you finally climb out, the desert has turned into a lush forest.

Now, open your eyes and write down the answers that the child gave you. This visualization exercise will guide you as to what hurt inside of you needs the divine feminine to heal and what sacred masculine steps you need to take to manifest the life you want.

Chapter 9: Tools for Healing Masculinity

The term wounded masculine refers to the negative impacts and manifestations of traditional gender roles and societal expectations on men's emotional well-being. Adhering strictly to conventional notions of masculinity and portraying qualities like emotional stoicism, dominance, and avoidance of vulnerability can lead to emotional and psychological distress.

Adhering strictly to conventional notions of masculinity can lead to emotional and psychological distress.
https://pixabay.com/photos/man-hike-sunset-hiker-mountaineer-1869135/

This chapter explores and addresses how these traditional expectations can harm you by suppressing your emotional expression and promoting a sense of inadequacy when it comes to understanding and dealing with emotions. The wounded masculine concept, in simple words, means that adhering rigidly to traditional gender roles can create emotional wounds and challenges for men that may hinder their overall well-being.

The goal here is to redefine these traditional notions of masculinity, encouraging a more inclusive and emotionally open understanding of what it means to be a man. This chapter offers practical strategies and insights to help men embrace vulnerability, heal from emotional wounds, and develop a healthier relationship with their emotions. The right shift in perspective can contribute to a more positive and holistic approach to masculinity, improving emotional well-being and personal growth.

Common Struggles

The struggles and signs associated with the wounded masculine can manifest in various ways. It's important to note that individuals may experience these challenges to varying degrees, and not everyone adheres strictly to traditional gender roles. Nevertheless, some everyday struggles and signs associated with the wounded masculine include:

Fear of Vulnerability

If you find it difficult to express your emotions openly, you may be experiencing the wounded masculine. There's often a deep-seated fear of showing vulnerability or perceived weakness. This fear might make it challenging to seek help or support, as acknowledging emotional struggles can be daunting.

Shame

The wounded masculine may lead to feelings of inadequacy or failure, often rooted in internalized shame for not meeting societal expectations of masculinity. It's important to recognize and address this shame, as it can significantly influence your self-perception and make it difficult to embrace your own flaws and imperfections.

Lack of Emotional Expression

If you notice a limited emotional range and struggle to express emotions like sadness, fear, or tenderness, you might be experiencing the wounded masculine. That can lead to disconnecting from your own emotional experiences and challenges in understanding and articulating your feelings.

Isolation

Do you find yourself withdrawing or emotionally isolating? The wounded masculine can hinder the formation of deep, meaningful connections due to the fear of vulnerability and difficulty expressing emotions. Building and maintaining healthy relationships may require addressing these challenges.

Distorted Sexual Energy

Challenges in forming intimate connections are common in the wounded masculine. Emotional barriers may impede genuine intimacy and connection, leading to unhealthy attitudes or behaviors related to sexuality. Transforming distorted sexual energy is a crucial aspect of the healing process.

Perfectionism

If you constantly need to prove your worth or competence and set unrealistically high standards, perfectionism associated with the wounded masculine may be at play. It's essential to recognize and navigate this perfectionistic mindset, including addressing the fear of failure and avoiding situations where success is not guaranteed.

Aggression or Hostility

Have you noticed yourself expressing frustration or emotional pain through aggression? That can be a common manifestation of the wounded masculine. Difficulty managing and channeling anger healthily may result in using aggression as a defense mechanism, impacting your well-being and relationships.

Lack of Direction and Motivation

Feeling lost or without a clear purpose is a hallmark of the wounded masculine. If you're struggling to set and pursue meaningful goals, exploring and discovering personal passions is essential. This exploration is crucial for overcoming a lack of motivation and enthusiasm for life.

Dependency on External Validation

Are you primarily seeking validation from external sources? The wounded masculine often relies on societal expectations or others' opinions for self-worth. Breaking free from this cycle of dependence is crucial for genuine self-acceptance and self-validation.

Avoidance of Introspection

If you find yourself avoiding self-reflection, conversations, or activities that prompt deeper self-exploration, it may be time to embrace introspection. The wounded masculine often involves reluctance to confront and address personal challenges. Taking steps toward introspection is a vital part of your journey toward healing and growth.

The Root Causes

As you read through, consider how these factors might resonate with your own experiences:

Childhood Trauma

The impact of childhood trauma is profound, shaping the sense of self and influencing behaviors. Experiences like physical, emotional, or sexual abuse, as well as neglect, can become internalized, giving rise to negative beliefs and coping mechanisms that significantly influence the understanding of masculinity.

Internalization of Negative Beliefs

It's typical for societal expectations and cultural norms to promote negative beliefs about oneself, particularly in the context of traditional masculinity.

Parental Wounds

The relationships you share with parents shape your identities. Strained connections with your father may leave you without a positive male role model, confusing healthy masculinity. Alternatively, challenging relationships with the mother can impact emotional well-being and affect how one navigates relationships.

Lack of a Positive Male Role Model

The absence of a positive male role model during formative years can leave a void where you lack clear guidance on healthy masculinity. This gap may drive anyone to identify their values in environments that reinforce traditional stereotypes. However, this pursuit can backfire and sometimes perpetuate harmful behaviors.

Societal Expectations and Gender Norms

Societal expectations regarding gender roles can exert significant pressure, contributing to wounded masculinity. The insistence on conforming to stereotypical masculine traits, like emotional stoicism and dominance, may lead to suppressing authentic emotions and developing a distorted sense of self.

Peer Pressure and Social Conditioning

Peer influence and societal conditioning play a crucial role in the development of wounded masculinity. The desire to fit in with peer groups or conform to societal norms can lead to the adoption of behaviors that align with traditional masculinity, even if they are detrimental to emotional well-being.

Media Representation

Media portrayal of masculinity is a powerful force that shapes perceptions. Often, media perpetuates narrow ideals and stereotypes, influencing how someone sees themselves. Unrealistic standards of strength, dominance, and success will only trigger negative behaviors and contribute to the development of wounded masculinity.

Reflecting on these factors can provide insight into your experiences and help you understand the influences that may have contributed to your perception of masculinity. By recognizing these root causes, you can carry on the journey of self-discovery and healing, seeking to redefine masculinity in a way that aligns with your authentic self.

Understanding Your Perception

It's a journey of self-reflection, a chance to untangle the threads of beliefs woven into the fabric of your identity. Here are some questions that might bring clarity to your experiences and, in doing so, create space for personal growth, healing, and transformation.

Childhood and Family Dynamics

Think back to your early years. What were the messages about being a man that echoed through your childhood home? How did the dynamics with your father or mother shape your understanding of masculinity? Sometimes, the roots of our beliefs go deep, and acknowledging them is the first step toward understanding.

Personal Beliefs and Conditioning

Consider the beliefs about masculinity you've absorbed from societal expectations and cultural norms. Have you ever found yourself conforming to traditional stereotypes, perhaps unknowingly? Or maybe you've resisted these expectations by forging your own path. Understanding your conditioned beliefs lays the groundwork for intentional self-discovery.

Emotional Expression and Vulnerability

Reflect on your relationship with emotions. How comfortable are you with expressing vulnerability? Have you ever felt the need to suppress certain emotions because they didn't align with societal notions of masculinity? Exploring these aspects can shed light on your emotional landscape.

Role Models and Influences

Who are the figures you've looked up to in terms of masculinity? How have they influenced your perception of being a man? Sometimes, role models shape ideals, knowingly or unknowingly, and examining their impact can reveal much about your own beliefs.

Peer and Social Influences

Think about your friends and social circles. In what ways have they influenced your understanding of masculinity? Have you ever felt pressured to conform to certain ideals to fit in? The social environment often plays a significant role in shaping identities.

Media Representation

Consider the role of media in your perception of masculinity. How have portrayals in movies, TV shows, or advertisements influenced how you see yourself? Have you ever compared yourself to media images of "ideal" masculinity, and how did that make you feel? Media holds a mirror to society, reflecting and shaping our perceptions.

Personal Growth and Healing

What outdated expectations about masculinity are you ready to let go of? How can embracing a more authentic and inclusive definition of masculinity contribute to your personal growth and healing? Recognizing the need for change is the first step toward transformation.

Relationships and Intimacy

Consider the impact of your perception of masculinity on your relationships, especially in terms of intimacy and emotional connection. Have societal expectations ever hindered your ability to be vulnerable in relationships? Understanding these dynamics can pave the way for more authentic connections.

Cultural and Societal Expectations

How do cultural or societal expectations about masculinity influence your choices in your daily life? Are there pressures you're ready to challenge or redefine in your understanding of being a man? Taking a critical look at these influences can empower you to shape your identity on your own terms.

Engaging with these questions isn't just a journey of reflection. It's a step towards understanding, growth, and self-empowerment. It's about letting go of societal pressures that no longer serve you and creating space for masculinity that aligns with your authentic self.

Mindfulness Meditation

Mindfulness meditation is a powerful practice that can significantly cultivate self-awareness and enhance emotional intelligence.

Understanding Mindfulness Meditation

Mindfulness meditation is rooted in ancient contemplative traditions, particularly in Buddhism, and has gained widespread recognition for its benefits in promoting mental well-being. At its core, mindfulness involves cultivating a heightened awareness and presence in the current moment.

Getting Started with Mindfulness Meditation

Find a Quiet Space

Choose a quiet and comfortable space where you won't be disturbed. That could be a corner of your room, a park, or any place where you can sit or lie down comfortably.

Assume a Comfortable Posture

Sit in a comfortable position with your back straight. You can sit on a chair or cushion, cross-legged on the floor, or even lie down. The key is to maintain a posture that is both relaxed and alert.

Focus on Your Breath

Begin by bringing your attention to your breath. Notice the sensation of each inhalation and exhalation. You can focus on the rise and fall of your chest or the sensation of air passing through your nostrils.

Cultivate Present-Moment Awareness

As you breathe, let your attention rest entirely on the present moment. Notice any thoughts, sensations, or emotions that arise without judgment. The goal is not to eliminate thoughts but to observe them with curiosity and non-judgmental awareness.

Bring Attention Back to the Breath

When your mind inevitably wanders (as it naturally does), gently guide your attention back to your breath. This process of redirecting your focus helps strengthen your ability to stay present.

Body Scan Meditation (Optional)

Another mindfulness technique involves a body scan, systematically bringing your attention to different body parts, observing sensations, and promoting relaxation.

Benefits of Mindfulness Meditation

Increased Self-Awareness

Mindfulness meditation encourages a deep connection with your thoughts, emotions, and bodily sensations. Regularly observing your mental landscape, you develop a heightened self-awareness, recognizing patterns and understanding your inner world more profoundly.

Emotional Regulation

Mindfulness helps in recognizing and processing emotions as they arise. By observing emotions without immediate reaction or judgment, you can respond skillfully to situations, promoting emotional regulation and balance.

Enhanced Concentration and Focus

The practice of mindfulness strengthens your ability to concentrate on the present moment. This heightened focus extends to your daily activities, improving your attention span and overall cognitive performance.

Stress Reduction

Mindfulness has been shown to reduce stress by promoting relaxation and cultivating a non-reactive awareness of stressors. This, in turn, contributes to better emotional well-being.

Improved Interpersonal Relationships

Mindfulness meditation positively impacts your interactions with others by fostering self-awareness and emotional intelligence. You become more attuned to the emotions of those around you, enhancing empathy and communication skills.

Integrating Mindfulness into Daily Life

Start Small

Begin with short sessions, perhaps 5-10 minutes, and gradually increase the duration as you become more comfortable with the practice.

Consistency Is Key

Regularity is more important than duration. Aim for daily practice to experience the cumulative benefits of mindfulness.

Mindful Activities

Extend mindfulness to daily activities such as eating, walking, or washing dishes. Engage fully in these moments, bringing your attention to the present.

Mindfulness Apps and Resources

Consider using mindfulness apps that offer guided meditations. These tools can provide structure and support, especially if you're new to the practice.

Remember, mindfulness meditation is a journey, not a destination. Be patient with yourself and approach the practice with a gentle and compassionate mindset. As you cultivate self-awareness and emotional intelligence through mindfulness, you'll likely find it a valuable resource for navigating life's challenges with greater ease and clarity.

Expressing Emotions

Expressing emotions healthily and assertively is a crucial aspect of emotional well-being. Here are some insights and practical tips to help readers articulate their feelings and vulnerabilities without associating them with weakness:

Understanding Assertiveness

Assertiveness involves expressing your thoughts, feelings and needs clearly and respectfully while respecting the rights and boundaries of others. It's about finding a balance between being open and honest without being passive or aggressive.

Identify and Acknowledge Your Emotions

Start by recognizing and acknowledging your emotions. Understand that all feelings are valid and natural. Whether joy, sadness, frustration, or vulnerability, each emotion conveys essential information about your inner experience.

Use "I" Statements

When expressing your feelings or vulnerabilities, frame your statements using "I" statements. For example, instead of saying, "You always do this," say, "I feel frustrated when this happens." That helps you take ownership of your emotions and avoids sounding accusatory.

Be Specific

Provide specific details about your feelings or vulnerabilities. This clarity helps others understand your perspective and facilitates more effective communication. Instead of saying, "I'm upset about everything," specify the particular actions or situations that bother you.

Practice Active Listening

Developing assertiveness involves not only expressing yourself but also actively listening to others. When in a conversation, make an effort to understand the other person's perspective. That creates a supportive environment for open communication.

Set Boundaries

Clearly define your boundaries and communicate them assertively. Let others know what behaviors are acceptable and unacceptable to you. That helps with establishing healthy and respectful relationships.

Choose the Right Time and Place

Timing and environment matter. Choose a suitable time and place for expressing your feelings, especially if the matter is sensitive. That ensures you and the other person can engage in the conversation without unnecessary distractions or pressures.

Practice Self-Compassion

Recognize that expressing vulnerabilities is a sign of strength, not weakness. Practice self-compassion by acknowledging that everyone has vulnerabilities and it's okay to share them. Treat yourself with the same kindness you would offer to a friend.

Seek Solutions

When expressing your feelings, be open to discussing potential solutions or compromises. This proactive approach demonstrates a willingness to work together and find resolutions rather than venting frustrations.

Use Positive Affirmations

Integrate positive affirmations into your self-talk. Remind yourself that expressing emotions and vulnerabilities is a courageous and healthy act. Affirmations can help reshape negative beliefs about assertiveness.

Seek Support

If expressing your emotions feels challenging, consider seeking support from friends, family, or a mental health professional. They can provide guidance and encouragement as you develop and practice assertive communication skills.

Remember, being assertive is about fostering healthy communication and relationships. It's a skill that can be developed with practice, and over time, it contributes to a more authentic and fulfilling way of expressing emotions without associating them with weakness. Embracing assertiveness can lead to more meaningful connections and greater empowerment in navigating life's challenges.

This chapter has been a journey into understanding and embracing a more authentic and holistic approach to masculinity. It started by exploring the concept of the "wounded masculine," recognizing the negative impacts of traditional gender roles on men's emotional well-being. By identifying struggles such as fear of vulnerability, shame, and distorted sexual energy, the aim was to shed light on the challenges that many individuals face in adhering strictly to societal expectations.

You've already explored the root causes of wounded masculinity, examining factors such as childhood trauma, internalization of negative beliefs, mother/father wounds, and the absence of positive male role models. Recognizing these influences is crucial for initiating a process of healing and personal growth.

Lastly, you were introduced to mindfulness meditation as a powerful tool for cultivating self-awareness and emotional intelligence. Practicing mindfulness can deepen your connection with yourself, regulate emotions, and navigate life's challenges with greater resilience. From mindfulness meditation to assertive expression of emotions, the chapter provided a toolbox for fostering emotional well-being, self-awareness, and personal growth.

As you reflect on what you've learned, remember that the journey toward a healthier masculinity is ongoing. It involves self-compassion, openness to growth, and a commitment to reshaping your relationship with yourself and the world around you. Embrace the insights gained in this chapter as you navigate the path toward a more fulfilling and authentic expression of your masculinity.

Chapter 10: The Ever-Unfolding Path

The divine masculine does not stagnate. This means that the path toward your destiny in your masculine expression is ever-unfolding. The more you work towards your goals concerning your masculine energy, the more you discover about yourself. When carving out a new path, unfamiliar situations arise. The universal principles of divine masculinity allow you to navigate this darkness with the light of perseverance, awareness, and resilience. The sacred masculine path is a dynamic form of knowledge and wisdom because as you continue unfolding its mysteries, you become aware of how much more there is to discover. However, even with a limited intellectual understanding, the sacred masculine can be experienced through practical application.

The sacred masculine path is a dynamic form of knowledge and wisdom.
https://pixabay.com/photos/man-outdoors-monochrome-sunlight-3556090/

The unfolding path of the divine masculine is expansive, revealing new realities that can only be accessed through action. You can use your smartphone to search for information and gain knowledge through diligent study. True wisdom can only be achieved through hands-on experience. No matter how many karate books you read, you'll never understand martial arts until you step into the ring. Similarly, the divine masculine cannot be understood simply by reading this text. It has to be lived out through your journey of growth. The main takeaway that should be highlighted in your understanding of the divine masculine is to stop thinking about it and start doing it. Many talented individuals have been hindered by their fear of taking the first step. There was probably someone who existed in history who was ten times smarter than Albert Einstein, but his name has been forgotten because he never had the bravery to break through the barriers of fear and doubt. Go ahead and dive into the deep end because you'll either sink or swim, but either way, you'll learn a powerful lesson.

Your Personal Transformative Journey

Although the sacred masculine can be interpreted through a societal or even universal lens, the most relevant understanding of this powerful energy is how it relates to you internally. When you are transformed, your actions will change, influencing the community you are a part of. Masculine energy is a seed that cracks open the more you keep watering it with mindfulness, introspection, accountability, and action. Slowly, the roots of the seed begin to spread, and the plant breaks through the soil barrier where others can see the difference in your life. Eventually, the plant bears fruit, which is the point where you begin to reap the benefits of your efforts.

Much like a plant, this transformative journey takes time. Since masculine energy is the process of breaking free from thoughts and dreams into action, it is best to stay focused on the present moment and work on yourself daily. It can be difficult to restrain yourself from dwelling on the past or focusing too much on the future. Mindfulness is an amazing tool that opens the gateways to the sacred masculine. It is the practice of bringing your attention to the present moment by using various meditations and techniques.

Self-analysis and introspection are two more keys that unlock the floodgates of masculine energy. You cannot take informed action if you are operating in delusion. Introspection and self-awareness are ways in which you can be honest with yourself. Part of functioning in the divine masculine is assuming responsibility for where you find yourself and avoiding pointing the finger at others. There is no denying that people and events influence your life. However, you choose how you can respond to these hardships and changes. Responsibility, when you dissect the word, is the ability to respond. You never placed the potholes on the long road of transformation you are embarking on, but you are steering so you can swerve and dodge them. Even if you hit a pothole and flatten a tire, you can pull to the side of the road, gather yourself, change the wheel, and continue pushing forward.

The divine masculine does not baby you to dwell in the self-pity of a "woe is me" attitude. This does not mean you need to cut yourself off from your emotions and become a passionless, cold shell of a human. That is a distorted form of the sacred masculine that is not balanced. Feeling your emotions fully is essential to being whole, but you must find ways to rationally integrate your feelings in ways that benefit you and your community. It does not help to look at a homeless person on the side of the road and feel sad for them. Your feelings are not going to help them in any tangible way. Only once you use the sacred masculine to channel your emotions into action do they become useful in manifesting a better world for yourself and others.

New Insights and Understanding

Exploring archetypes and understanding how they manifest in you both negatively and positively will help you gain new insight into how you function. There is no one way to express the sacred masculine, so how it shows up in your life could completely differ from how you expected it to be. Furthermore, people consistently change, so the archetypes and expressions of masculine energy that served you in one phase may no longer be relevant as you grow. For example, with their battles and experiences, the warrior archetype could gain the wisdom to become a sage as they get older.

All archetypes are expressed in you. However, there are a few that stand out as dominant. Understanding all these narrative forms and the psychological origins that birthed them allows you to plug into the archetypes you need to engage with when they become relevant. For example, you may be working your way up the ladder at your job and receive a promotion into a leadership role. What once worked in your old position will no longer apply to your new one. You may find yourself having to dig into the non-dominant archetypes. By understanding each archetype's ins and outs, you can manifest the new energy needed for any new and uncovered roads.

It is difficult to place any human into a clear-cut box. Most people feel like they are in touch with themselves, but in reality, humans are great at self-delusion. The complexity of the human condition always leaves room for new methods of analysis to be uncovered and developed. Therefore, the tools like archetypal figures used to assess masculine energy are also limited. These narrative structures are helpful, but you should not feel tied to them like a prison. Instead, use them in combination with meditation and mindfulness to unveil the more personalized aspects of your sacred masculine expressions.

The journey through yourself to find what drives you is blurry, which is why feminine energy is seen as chaotic. The process of sorting through the chaos is the masculine revealing itself. The sacred masculine is a ship used for navigating the waters of your being, but the feminine energy is like the wind propelling your sails. You cannot control how the wind blows, but you can adjust your sails to take you in the direction you want to go. It is not always easy because that wind can batter your ship. However, through meditation exercises and journaling, you have to patch up any unexpected holes in the sails to remain on the right path. Sometimes, storms can take you way off your planned route, but self-awareness is the process of recalibrating your compass, checking your maps, and slowly steering your ship to get back on course.

Bringing Positive Change to Yourself and Your Community

The birth of the divine masculine within you is not selfish. When the sacred masculine is actualized, you'll become a benefit to your community and society at large. When you look at what many consider traditional masculine values, which extend out of the primitive, evolutionarily engrained divine masculine, you find that selflessness, giving, and protection all come up as core characteristics of masculinity. Due to the sacred masculine being expressed in the external world, the divine masculine must be communal. Humans are social creatures who organize themselves in hierarchies. The order and leadership that spring forth from the divine masculine must be concerned with the well-being of others.

Masculinity expressed in a self-centered way cannot be called divine. Masculinity should not be super focused on individual gain. The sacred masculine is an energy of giving, while the sacred feminine is the attraction energy of receiving. Your introduction should not strictly be focused on bettering yourself but must also include your role in the community. Essentially, your exploration of self is for you to find out what you deem worthy of giving your life for. This could be your family, country, or a cause near your heart. The sacred masculine is purpose-driven, and humans can only find purpose in connections with others as a social species.

The seeds you plant in the community will come back to feed you. Although you should not expect anything back from selfless service, there will inevitably be those you help along the way who will appreciate you enough to uplift you. As much as an individualistic culture tries to erase the strong bonds between people, the altruistic drive of humanity is deeply encoded into the species' ancestral heritage. Those who have actualized into the sacred masculine are guided by creating a better society for all, especially the weak and vulnerable.

Growing into the Sacred Masculine

Growing and developing into your sacred masculine energy is the most fulfilling journey you can choose to embark on. A life spent passively waiting is wasted. The sacred masculine compels you to go out and get what you want, and in this pursuit, endless lessons will be learned. If you have the privilege of making it to old age, the divine masculine is what shapes the stories you will tell to younger generations – as well as the tales that will be told about you. This is your hero's journey. With your work and good deeds, you carve out the mythology attached to your name for generations to come.

You will not transform overnight, so adjust your expectations accordingly. Take small but consistent steps to apply the plan you crafted with your meditations and self-analysis. It is not heated motivation that brings forward victory but slow and steady discipline. The divine masculine requires you to constantly be putting in the effort, even on days when you don't want to. An Olympic runner trains for years to achieve victory in a few seconds. Your moment in the sunshine will only come about from the dirt under your nails, from clawing to the top when no one is looking.

As technology gets humans away from real-life interaction, an epidemic of loneliness is developing. Connection is what creates meaning. The loneliness permeating Western culture can only be cured by re-embracing divine masculinity outside of strictly acquiring excessive wealth. Playing the game is not just about the points you get on the scoreboard. There is nothing wrong with the desire to achieve, but being present in your sacred masculine energy means savoring every moment of the construction process.

Looking at a tall building and marveling at it is moving, but imagine how it feels when the people who laid the bricks and poured the concrete look at it. The pleasure of a job well done is found in the struggle of the process. Lottery winners are quickly separated from their funds because they weren't earned, but if you put your blood, sweat, and tears into something, you'll appreciate it more. Masculine energy is designed to take on strain and embrace challenges. This journey will be difficult because walking through the mud of your internal struggle is one of the hardest tasks you can do. People avoid the internal work needed to grow the divine masculine and opt to drown it with pleasure-seeking and escapism. However, these short-term solutions to the struggle for meaning will always leave you feeling empty. Divine masculine action driven by introspective value development is the only tried and tested path to fulfillment.

Conclusion

Implementation is a fundamental aspect of the sacred masculine. Now that you are done reading this book, you must take action for the profound benefits of the sacred masculine to start appearing in your life. These philosophies, descriptions, and practical tools have no use if you don't put in an effort. Just go ahead and start. Overthinking is the thief of success. For masculine energy to be effective, it has to flow. You'll inevitably make mistakes, but you can only address those flaws once you have identified them through your actions.

As much as you emphasize the sacred masculine, ensuring that you don't neglect the divine feminine is just as important. The chaotic, abstract, irrational, nurturing, and emotional energy of the divine feminine heals you so you can be functional enough to move forward in your pursuit of masculine energy. Regardless of your gender identity, to express the fullness of being human, you must find a balance between these two primordial energies.

The journey is constantly unfolding. Masculine energy is as infinite as the universe. You can never tap into all of it in one sitting. Therefore, the journey of embracing the sacred masculine is persistent. One of the key markers of masculinity is that it moves straight from point A to point B. However, the energy never stagnates because it is all about going forward and accomplishing tasks, so once you are at point B, there will be a point C to get to next. When you are fully invested in your sacred masculine, you will be internally motivated to keep moving and elevating.

Sacred masculine energy is competitive, but it is key to remember that your biggest competition is yourself. If you spend too much time looking around at what the next person is doing, you will never be able to get the razor-sharp focus that the actualized masculine is founded upon. The universe does not reward those constantly turning their necks to look left and right, but it can unlock endless abundance if you keep your eyes on the target. When a runner is completing a 100-meter sprint, you'll seldom see them looking at their competitors because if they stop focusing on the finish line, they will lose, so always keep your unwavering concentration.

Some of the meditative and introspective activities outlined in the book will not work if you only do them once. As you progress in your journey, revisit some concepts and exercises to measure where you are at. The sacred masculine is rational, so constant analysis of yourself in relation to where you once were reveals how far you've come and how far you still need to go.

Here's another book by Mari Silva that you might like

Your Free Gift
(only available for a limited time)

Thanks for getting this book! If you want to learn more about various spirituality topics, then join Mari Silva's community and get a free guided meditation MP3 for awakening your third eye. This guided meditation mp3 is designed to open and strengthen ones third eye so you can experience a higher state of consciousness. Simply visit the link below the image to get started.

https://spiritualityspot.com/meditation

Or, Scan the QR code!

References

Alethia. (2018, March 4). 9 Ways to Awaken the Divine Masculine Within You. LonerWolf. https://lonerwolf.com/divine-masculine/

Anderson, R. (2023, July 26). The Collective Consciousness of Divine Masculine and Feminine Energies. Www.linkedin.com. https://www.linkedin.com/pulse/collective-consciousness-divine-masculine-feminine-robert-anderson

Atsma, A. J. (2017). Aphrodite Myths 5 Loves - Greek Mythology. Theoi.com. https://www.theoi.com/Olympios/AphroditeLoves.html

Brett. (2011, October 4). The Four Archetypes of the Mature Masculine: The Lover. The Art of Manliness. https://www.artofmanliness.com/character/behavior/the-four-archetypes-of-the-mature-masculine-the-lover/

Brown, S. (2020, September 1). The Divine Masculine and the End of Patriarchy. Curious. https://medium.com/curious/the-divine-masculine-and-the-end-of-patriarchy-5c1c173f906f

Buffalmano, L. (2020, August 9). King, Warrior, Magician, Lover: The 4 Archetypes of Masculinity | TPM. Power DynamicsTM. https://thepowermoves.com/king-warrior-magician-lover/

Cherry, K. (2022, December 16). The 4 Major Jungian Archetypes. Verywell Mind; Verywellmind. https://www.verywellmind.com/what-are-jungs-4-major-archetypes-2795439

Cherry, K. (2023, June 9). Yin and Yang: How Ancient Ideas of Balance Can Help You. Verywell Mind. https://www.verywellmind.com/yin-and-yang-mental-health-7110781

Complex. (2011, August 16). The 10 Craziest Hacks Done By Anonymous. Complex. https://www.complex.com/pop-culture/a/complex/the-10-craziest-anonymous-hacks

Davenport, B. (2022, November 3). 7 Must-Know Masculine Energy Traits with Examples. Live Bold and Bloom. https://liveboldandbloom.com/11/self-improvement/masculine-energy-traits

Divine Masculine Energy: Traits, Balance, and Awakening - Centre of Excellence. (2023, December 27). Www.centreofexcellence.com. https://www.centreofexcellence.com/what-is-the-divine-masculine

Duarte, M. O. (2018, December 1). 12 Jungian Archetypes. Monica O. Duarte. https://monicaoduarte.com/meet-the-12-jungian-archetypes

Eisler, M. (2017, March 10). Laughter Meditation: 5 Healing Benefits and a 10-Minute Practice. Chopra. https://chopra.com/blogs/meditation/laughter-meditation-5-healing-benefits-and-a-10-minute-practice

Farah, S. (2015, February 4). The Archetypes of the Anima and Animus - Appliedjung. Appliedjung. https://appliedjung.com/the-archetypes-of-the-anima-and-animus/

Frawley, D. (n.d.). Understanding Prana. Yogainternational.com. https://yogainternational.com/article/view/understanding-prana/

Get Enough Sleep. (n.d.). Health.gov. https://health.gov/myhealthfinder/healthy-living/mental-health-and-relationships/get-enough-sleep

Gibson, L. (2022, May 4). Have a Problem? Ask Yourself 5 Questions. Mission Possible Strategies. https://missionpossiblestrategies.com/5-questions-to-ask-when-you-have-a-problem/

Gordon, S. (2023, October 5). What Is Grounding? Health. https://www.health.com/grounding-7968373

Gray, A. (2023, May 2). Divine Masculine Energy Traits - 10 Signs. The Invisible Man. https://www.the-invisibleman.com/path/what-is-divine-masculine-energy

Gray, A. (n.d.). Wounded Masculine Energy and Its Essence. The Invisible Man. https://www.the-invisibleman.com/path/what-is-wounded-masculine-energy-exactly

Harris, T. (n.d.). Enhancing Communication with Divine Masculine and Feminine Energies. Buyfromtj. https://www.buyfromtj.com/blog/enhancing-communication-with-divine-masculine-and-feminine-energies

Hilburn, S. (2021, May 28). The Rise of Divine Masculine. Conscious Community Magazine. https://consciouscommunitymagazine.com/the-rise-of-divine-masculine/

Jannyca. (2022, January 31). Embodied Yoga: 3 Ways to "Listen to Your Body" in Yoga. YogaUOnline. https://yogauonline.com/yoga-health-benefits/yoga-for-stress-relief/embodied-yoga-3-ways-to-listen-to-your-body-in-yoga

Jay, S. (2022, October 4). What Is Divine Masculine Energy + 19 Ways to Awaken Your Fire. Revoloon. https://revoloon.com/shanijay/divine-masculine-energy

JimLockard. (2019, September 1). Root Cause: Healing the Wounded Masculine Consciousness, Part 1. New Thought Evolutionary. https://newthoughtevolutionary.wordpress.com/2019/09/01/root-cause-healing-the-wounded-masculine-consciousness-part-1/

Jones, D. (2022, March 29). Mysticism of the Breath. Spirituality+Health. https://www.spiritualityhealth.com/mysticism-of-the-breath

Levesque, A. (2023, June 26). Divine Union: Weaving the Divine Masculine and Divine Feminine. Chaos & Light. https://chaosandlight.com/divine-union/

Lurey, D. (2014, October 9). The Lover - Archetypes of Men. Ekhart Yoga. https://www.ekhartyoga.com/articles/philosophy/the-lover-archetypes-of-men

Lurey, D. (2015, December 16). The Magician - Archetypes of Men. Ekhart Yoga. https://www.ekhartyoga.com/articles/practice/the-magician-archetypes-of-men

Maden, J. (2023). I Think Therefore I Am: Descartes' Cogito Ergo Sum Explained. Philosophybreak.com; Philosophy Break. https://philosophybreak.com/articles/i-think-therefore-i-am-descartes-cogito-ergo-sum-explained/

Main, P. (2023, March 30). Carl Jung's Archetypes. Www.structural-learning.com. https://www.structural-learning.com/post/carl-jungs-archetypes

McCartney, T. (2021, March 18). The Power of Our Breath. Emissaries of Divine Light. https://emissaries.org/the-power-of-our-breath/

Meloy, R. S. (2019, April 24). Balancing Our Feminine and Masculine Energy. Pause Meditation. https://www.pausemeditation.org/single-post/balancing-feminine-masculine-energy

Mindful Staff. (2020, July 8). What Is Mindfulness? Mindful. https://www.mindful.org/what-is-mindfulness/

Oldale, R. J. (2020, September 2). Psychology 101: The 12 Major Archetypes and Their Shadows. Master Mind Content - Master Mind Master Life. https://mastermindcontent.co.uk/psychology-101-the-12-major-archetypes-and-their-shadows/

OVO. (2018). Brand Archetypes - What Are They? Carl Jung's Archetypes as Brands. OVO. https://brandsbyovo.com/expertise/brand-archetypes/

Raypole, C. (2019, May 24). 30 Grounding Techniques to Quiet Distressing Thoughts. Healthline. https://www.healthline.com/health/grounding-techniques

Regan, S. (2021, February 22). These 7 Ancient Laws Can Help You Improve Your Life & Empower Yourself. Mindbodygreen. https://www.mindbodygreen.com/articles/7-hermetic-principles

Regula, deTraci. (2019, June 30). Medusa's Curse: Greek Mythology. ThoughtCo. https://www.thoughtco.com/greek-mythology-medusa-1524415

Resnick, S. (n.d.). Dr. Stella Resnick Psychologist Embodiment Exercises. Dr Stella Resnick. https://www.drstellaresnick.com/embodiment-exercises

Sarah Bence, O. (2023, June 14). Grounding: Its Meaning, Benefits, and Exercises to Try. Verywell Health. https://www.verywellhealth.com/grounding-7494652

Schaffer, A. (2021, October 11). Analysis | Hacktivists are back. Washington Post. https://www.washingtonpost.com/politics/2021/10/11/hacktivists-are-back/

Scruggs-Hussein, T. (2021, August 17). A 12-Minute Meditation to Set the Tone for Your Leadership. Mindful; Mindful.org. https://www.mindful.org/a-12-minute-meditation-to-set-the-tone-for-your-leadership/

Shambo, S. (2023, March 13). 8 Ways to Develop Masculine Energy: Be Irresistible to Women. Tantric Academy. https://tantricacademy.com/masculine-energy/

Shiva and Kali: The Tantric Symbolism. (n.d.). Isha.sadhguru.org. https://isha.sadhguru.org/mahashivratri/shiva/shiva-kali-the-tantric-symbolism/

Sinatra, S. T., Sinatra, D. S., Sinatra, S. W., & Chevalier, G. (2023). Grounding – The Universal Anti-Inflammatory Remedy. Biomedical Journal, 46(1), 11-16. https://doi.org/10.1016/j.bj.2022.12.002

Spiritual Meditation. (2023, September 26). Www.uh.edu. https://www.uh.edu/adbruce/wellness/spiritual-meditation/

TemplePurohit. (2022, February 3). TemplePurohit. https://www.templepurohit.com/shiva-shakti-divine-union-consciousness-energy/

The Holy Bible, New International Version. (1984). Grand Rapids: Zondervan Publishing House

Wong, C. (2021, April 8). Mindfulness Meditation. Verywell Mind; Verywellmind. https://www.verywellmind.com/mindfulness-meditation-88369

You Struggle to Sit Still. (2022, October 3). The Times of India. https://timesofindia.indiatimes.com/life-style/relationships/love-sex/signs-your-masculinity-is-wounded/photostory/94539880.cms?picid=94539905

Your Headspace Mindfulness & Meditation Experts. (2023, October 13). What Is a Flow State, and What Are Its Benefits? Headspace. https://www.headspace.com/articles/flow-state

Yuan, L. (2022, January 3). Guide: 12 Jungian Archetypes as Popularized by the Hero and the Outlaw | Personality Psychology. Personality-Psychology.com. https://personality-psychology.com/guide-12-jungian-archetypes/

www.ingramcontent.com/pod-product-compliance
Lightning Source LLC
Chambersburg PA
CBHW051849160426
43209CB00006B/1217